fetish

/ˈfɛtɪʃ/

noun

1. 1.

a form of sexual desire in which gratification is linked to an abnormal degree to a particular object, item of clothing, part of the body, etc.

"a man with **a fetish for** surgical masks"

synonyms:
fixation, sexual fixation, obsession, compulsion, mania;
weakness, fancy, taste, fascination, craze, fad;
idée fixe;
informal thing, hang-up
"he developed a rubber fetish"

-

- 2.

an inanimate object worshipped for its supposed magical powers or because it is considered to be inhabited by a spirit.

synonyms:
juju, talisman, charm, amulet;
totem, icon, idol, image, effigy, doll, statue, figure, figurine;
archaic periapt
"he worshipped an African fetish"

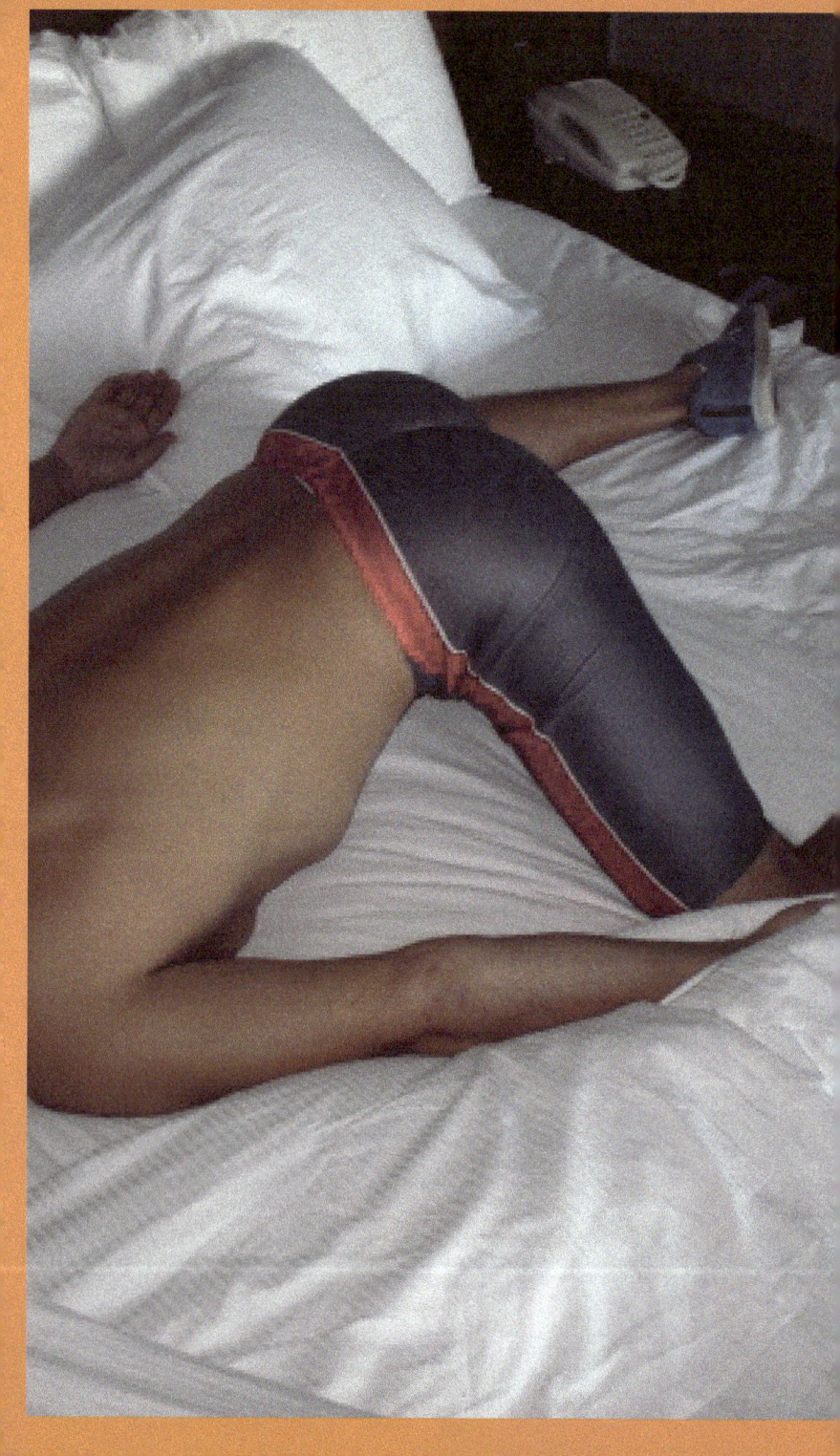

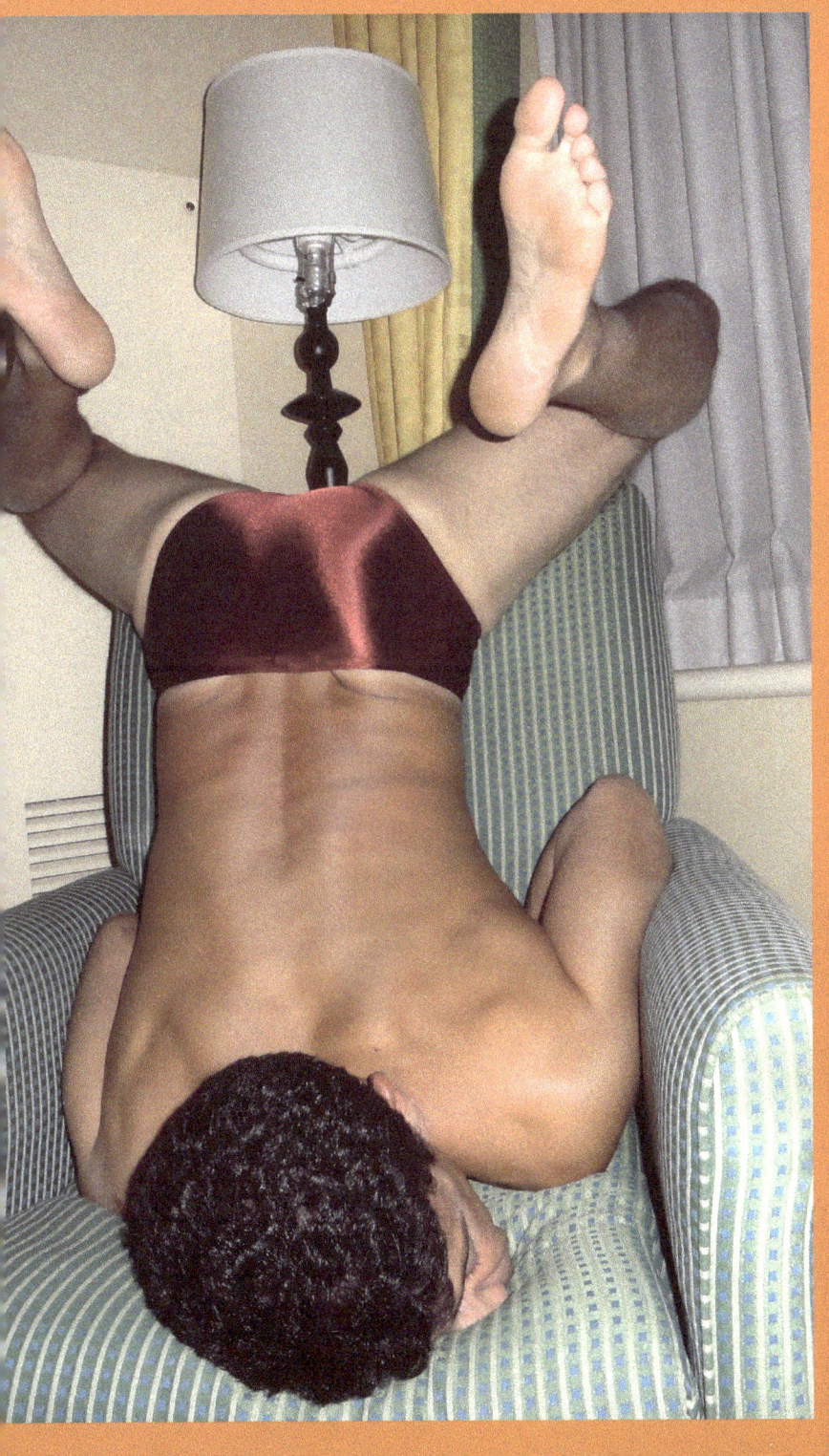

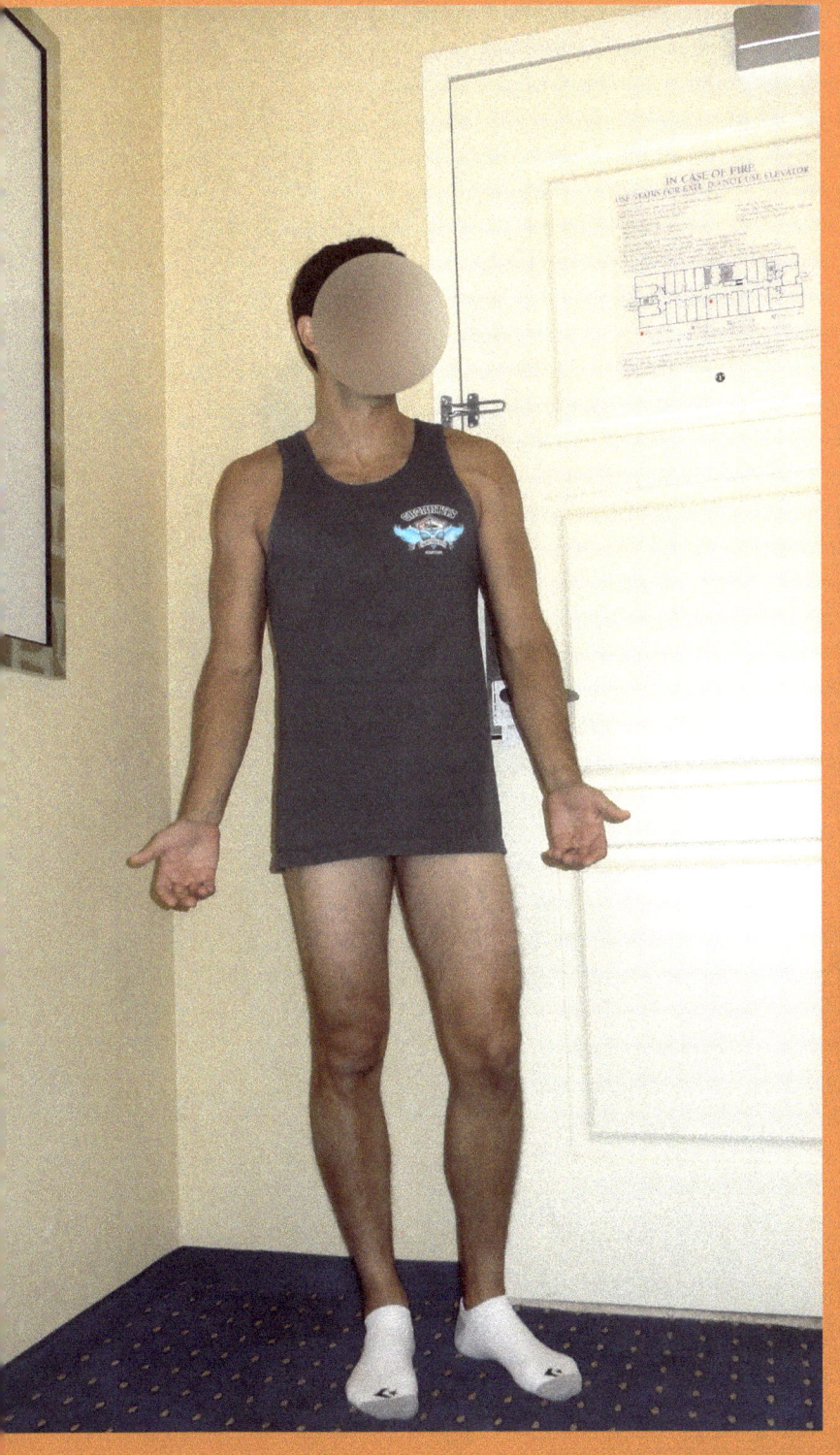

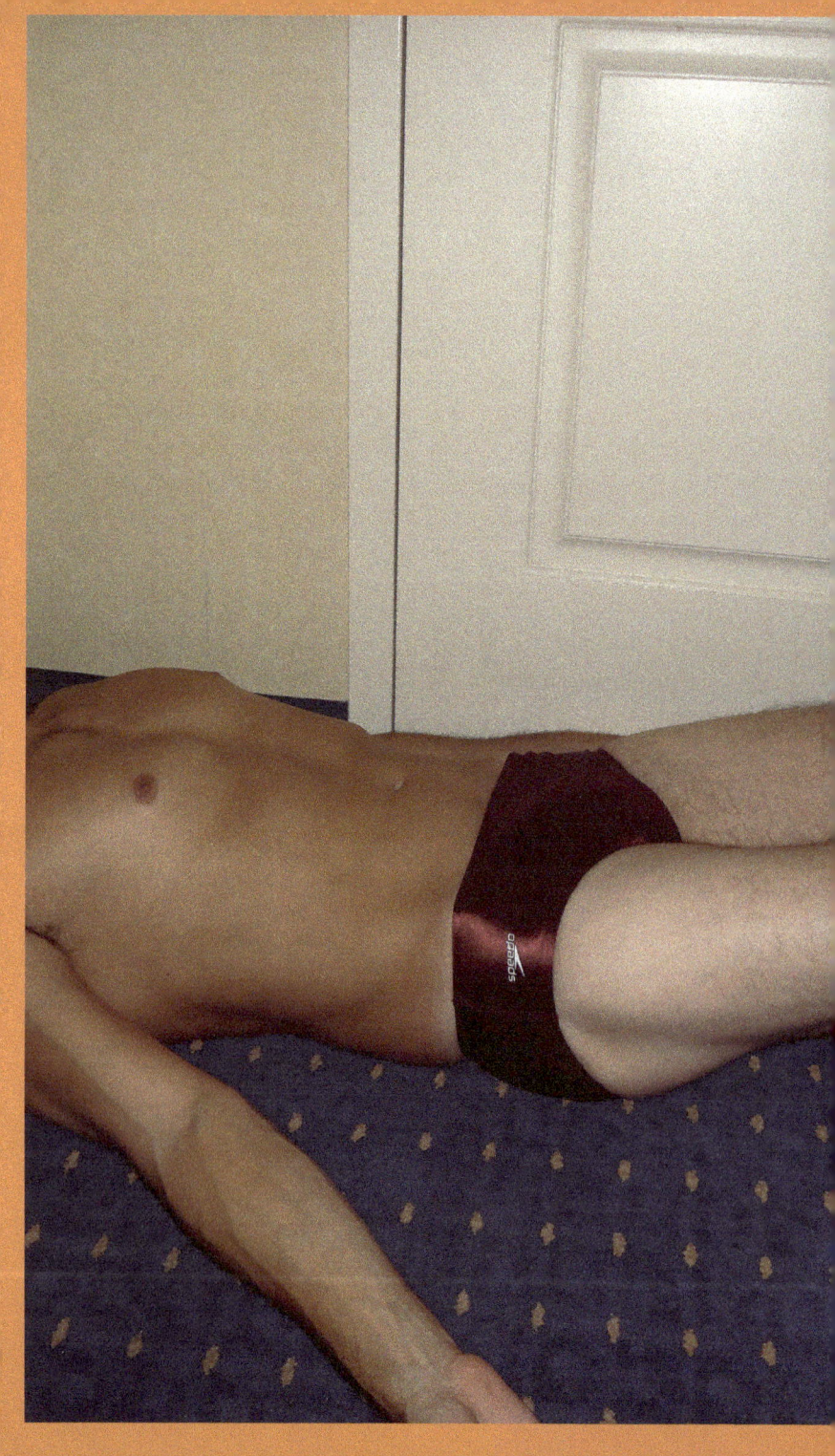

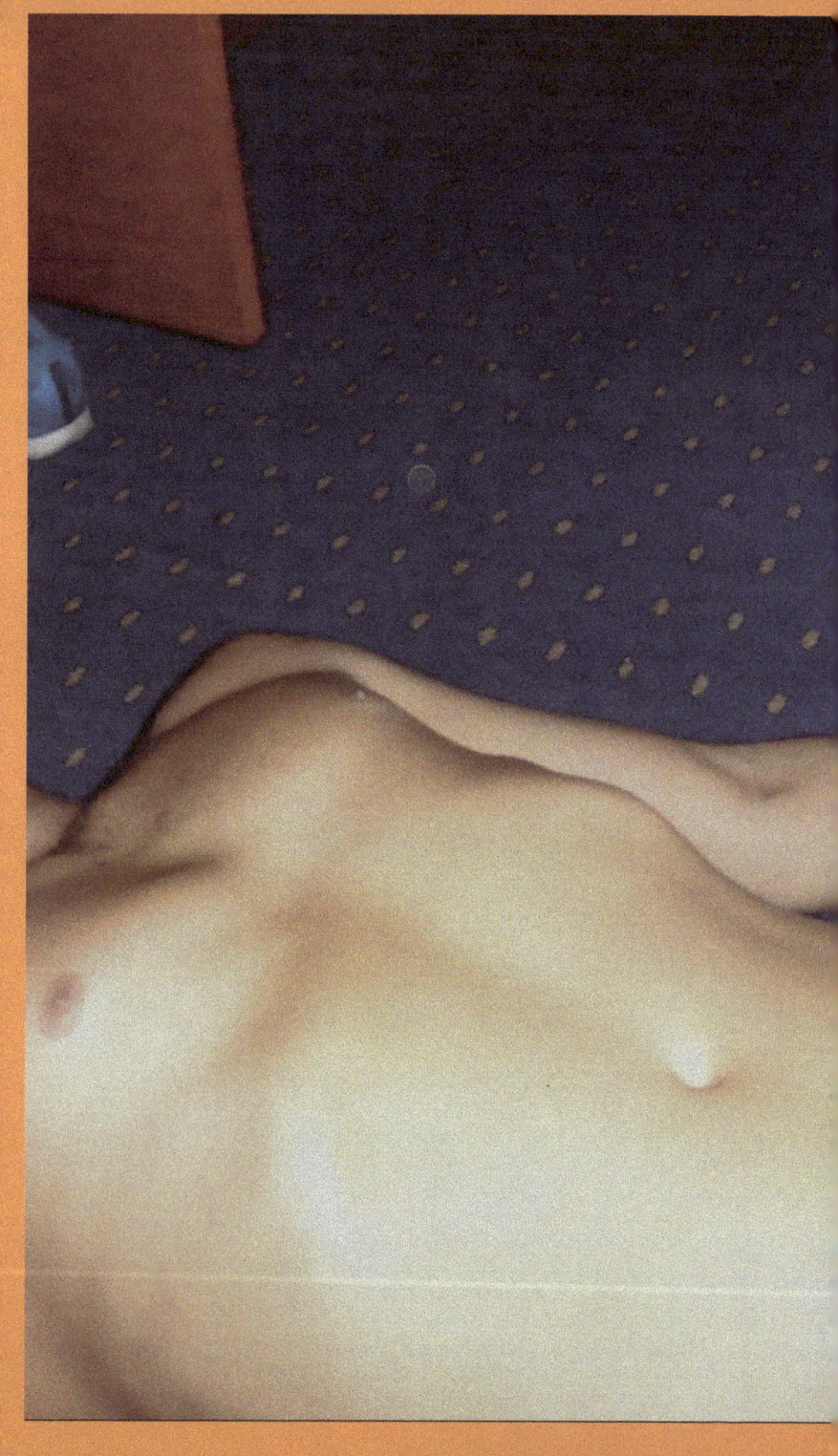

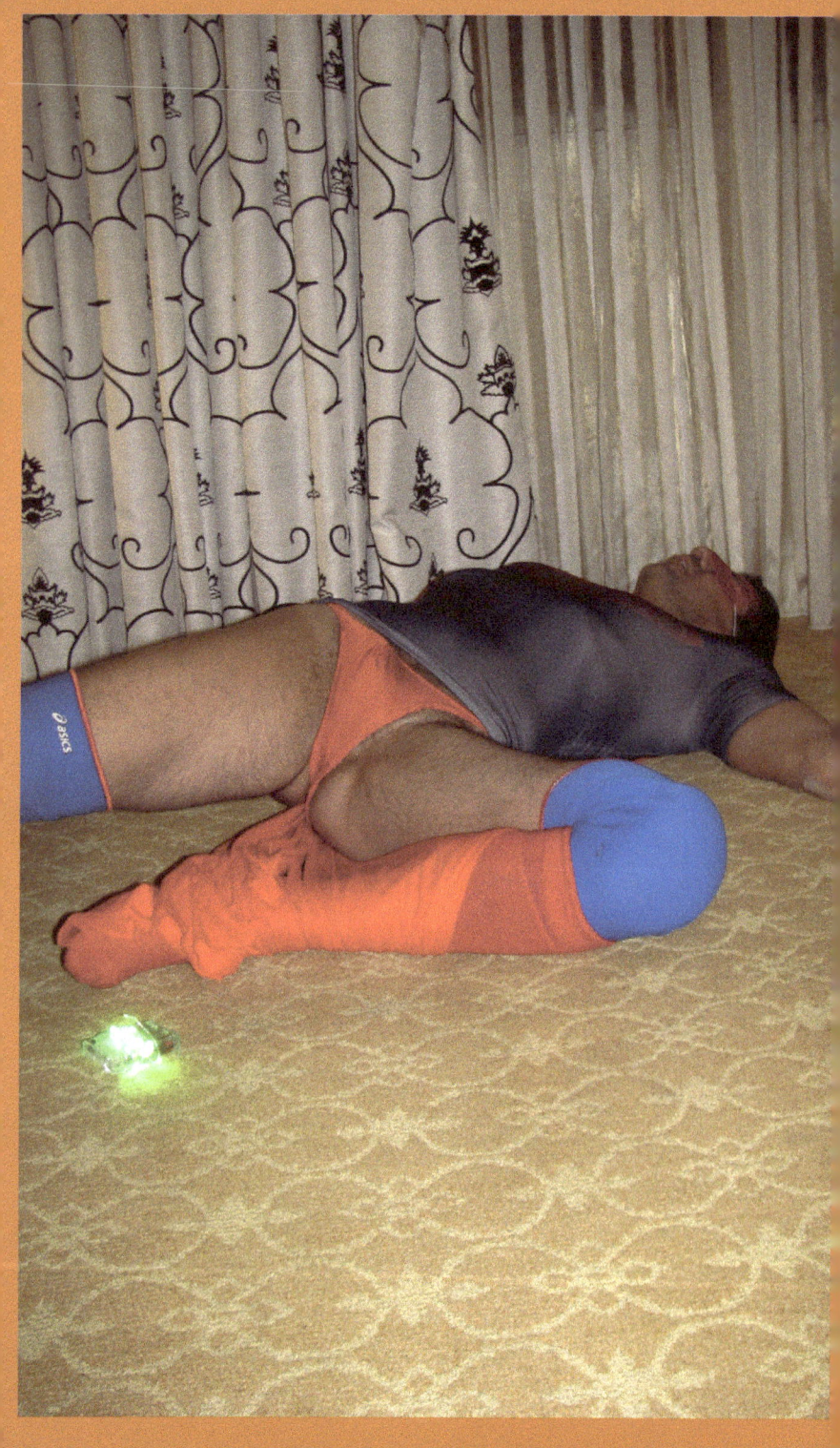

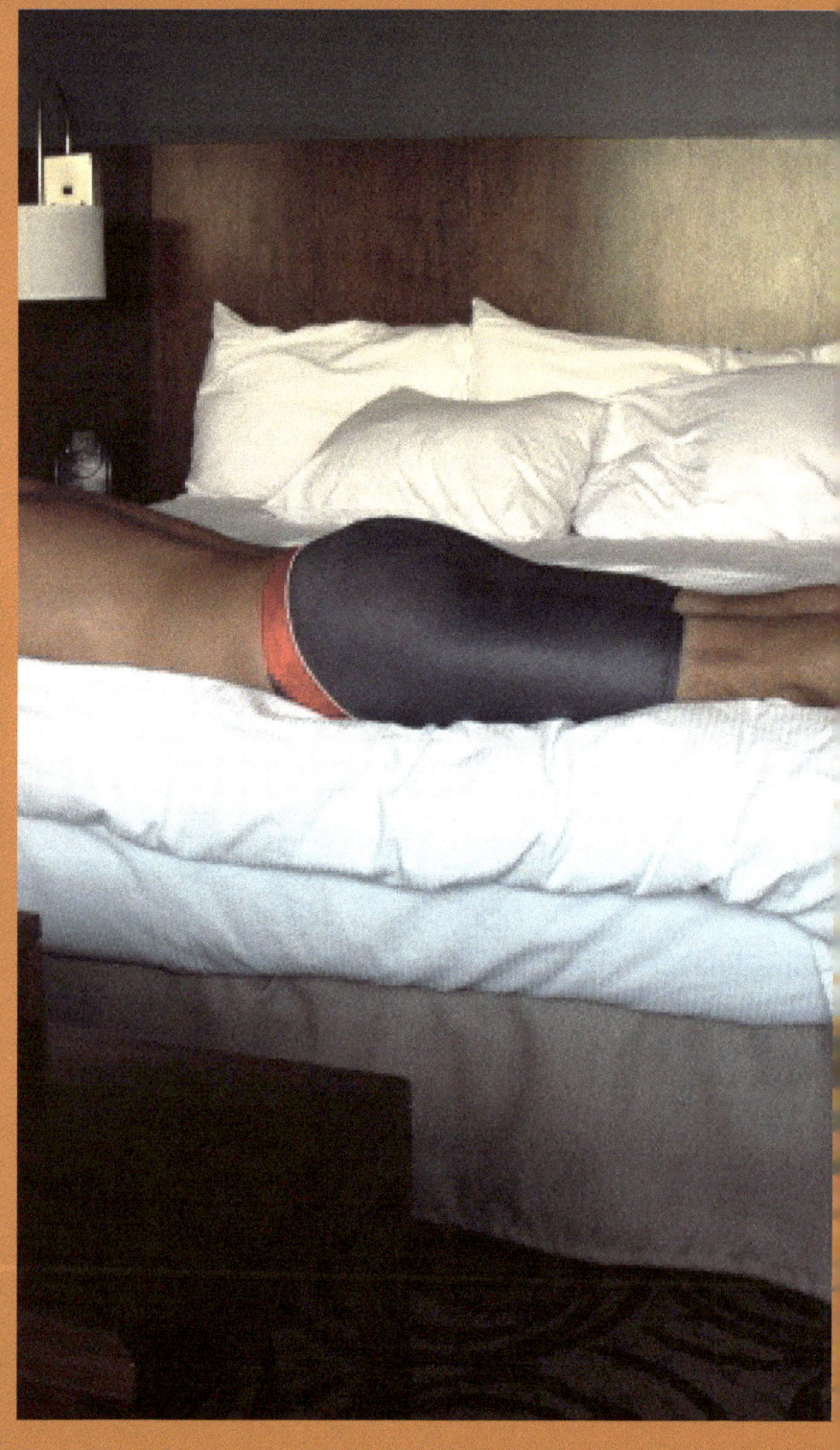

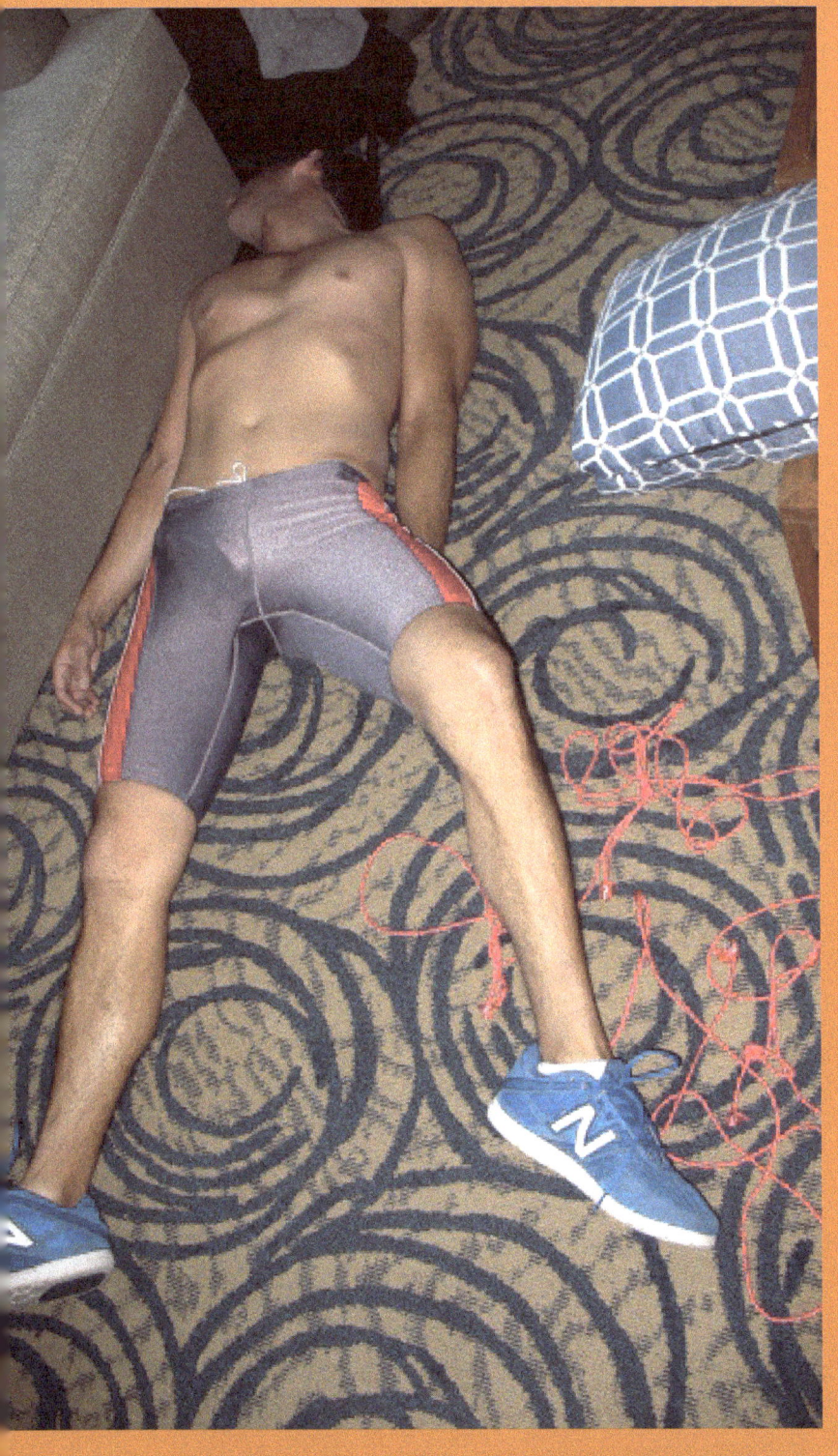

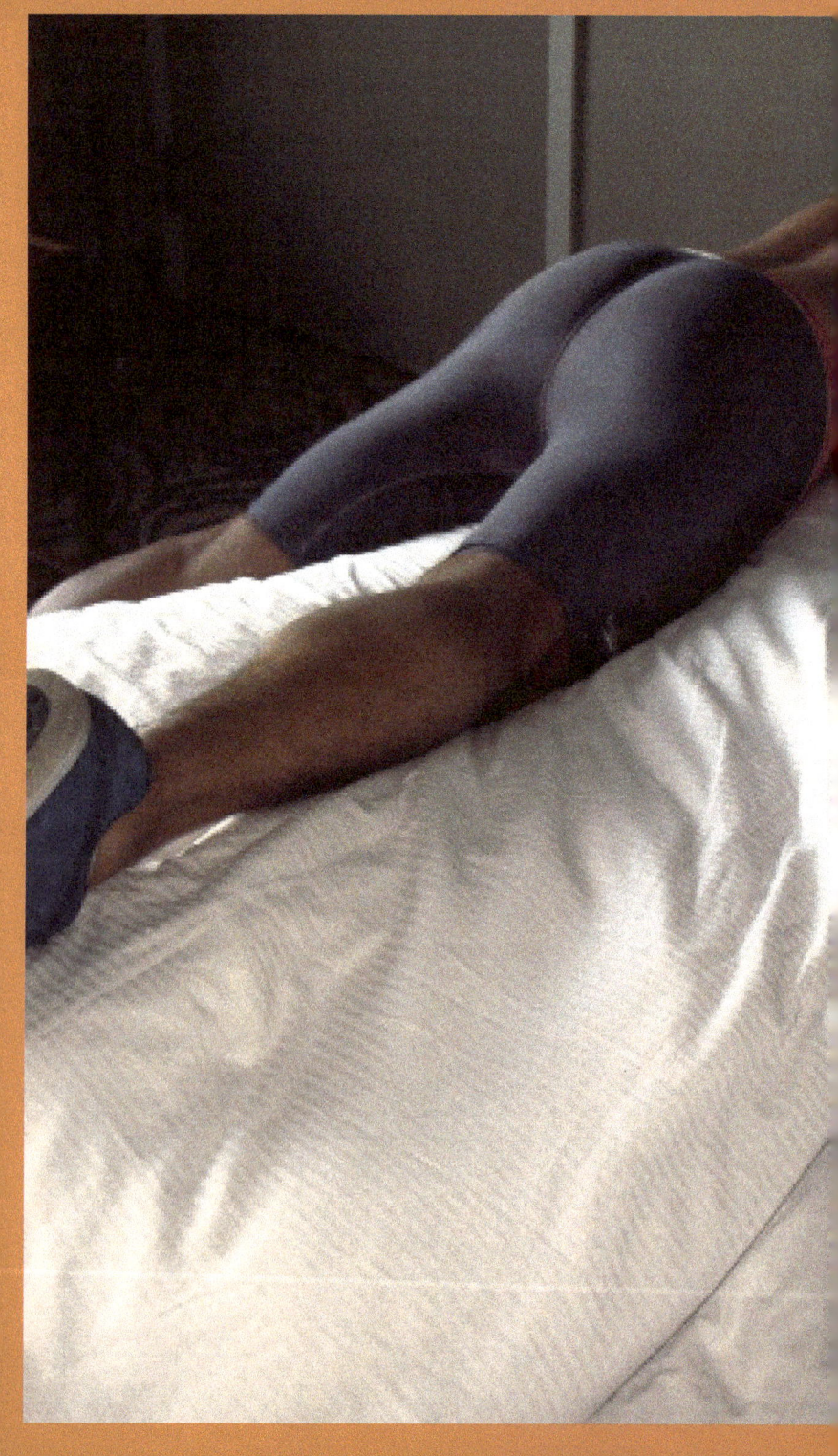

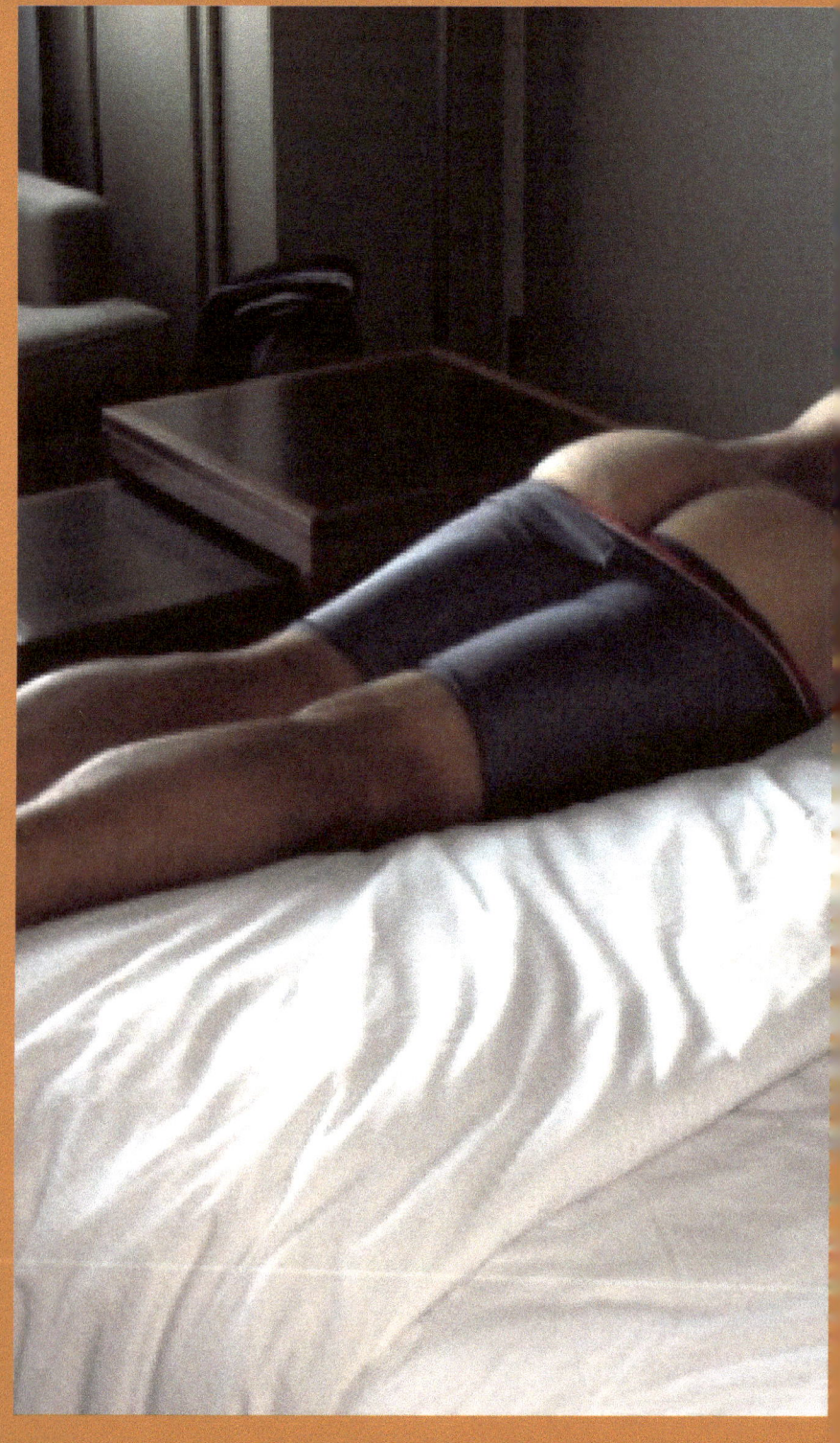

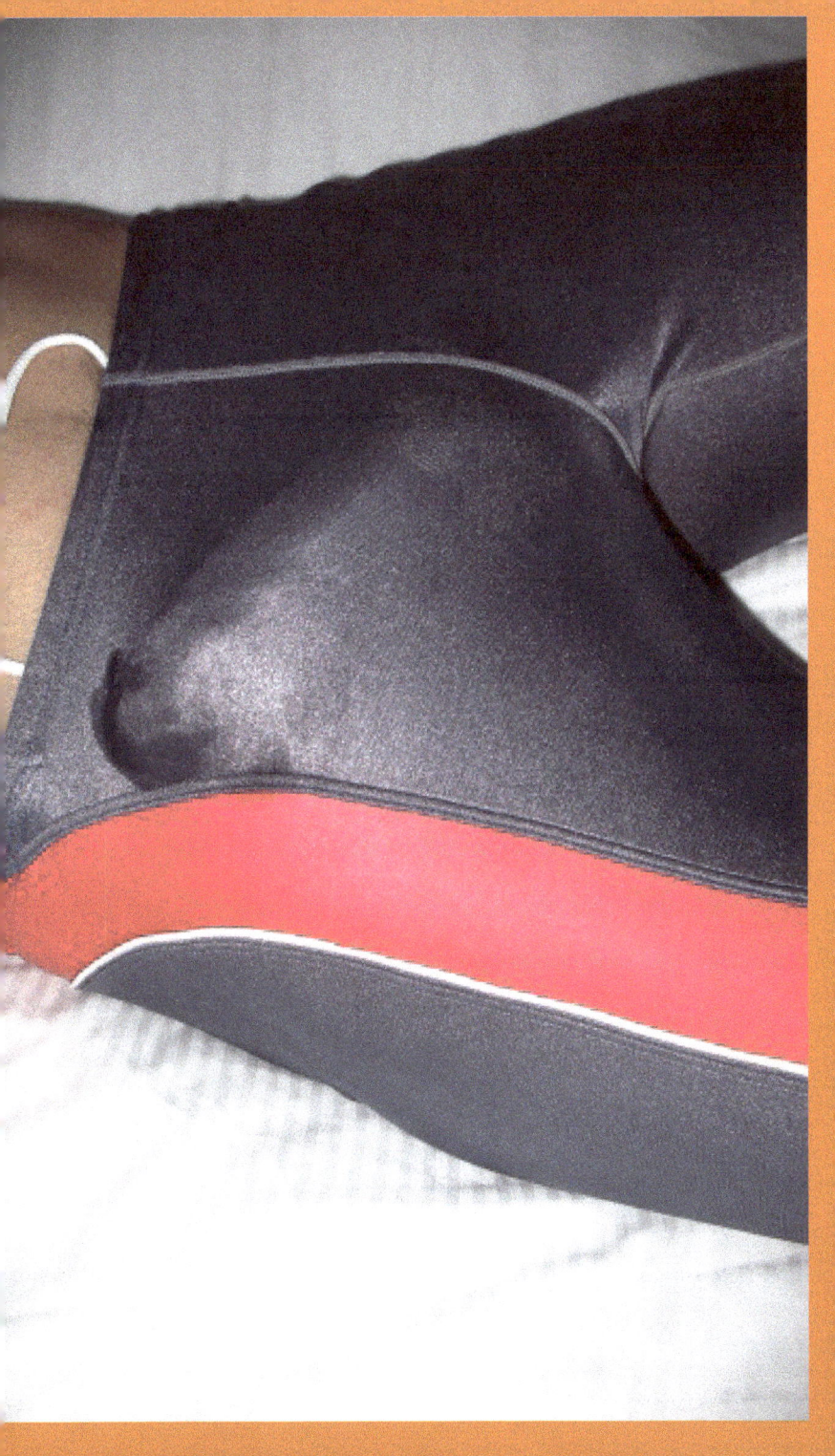

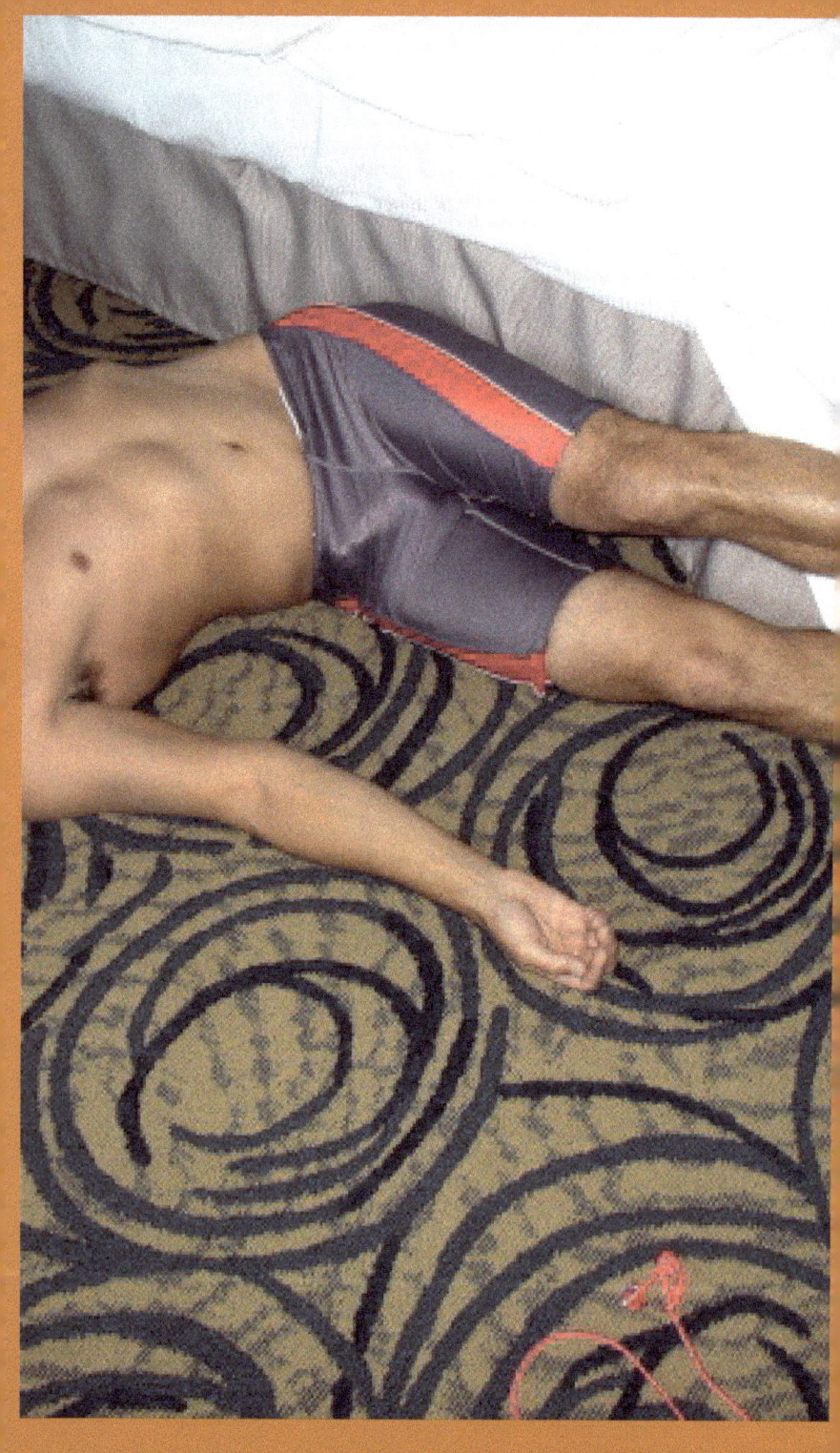

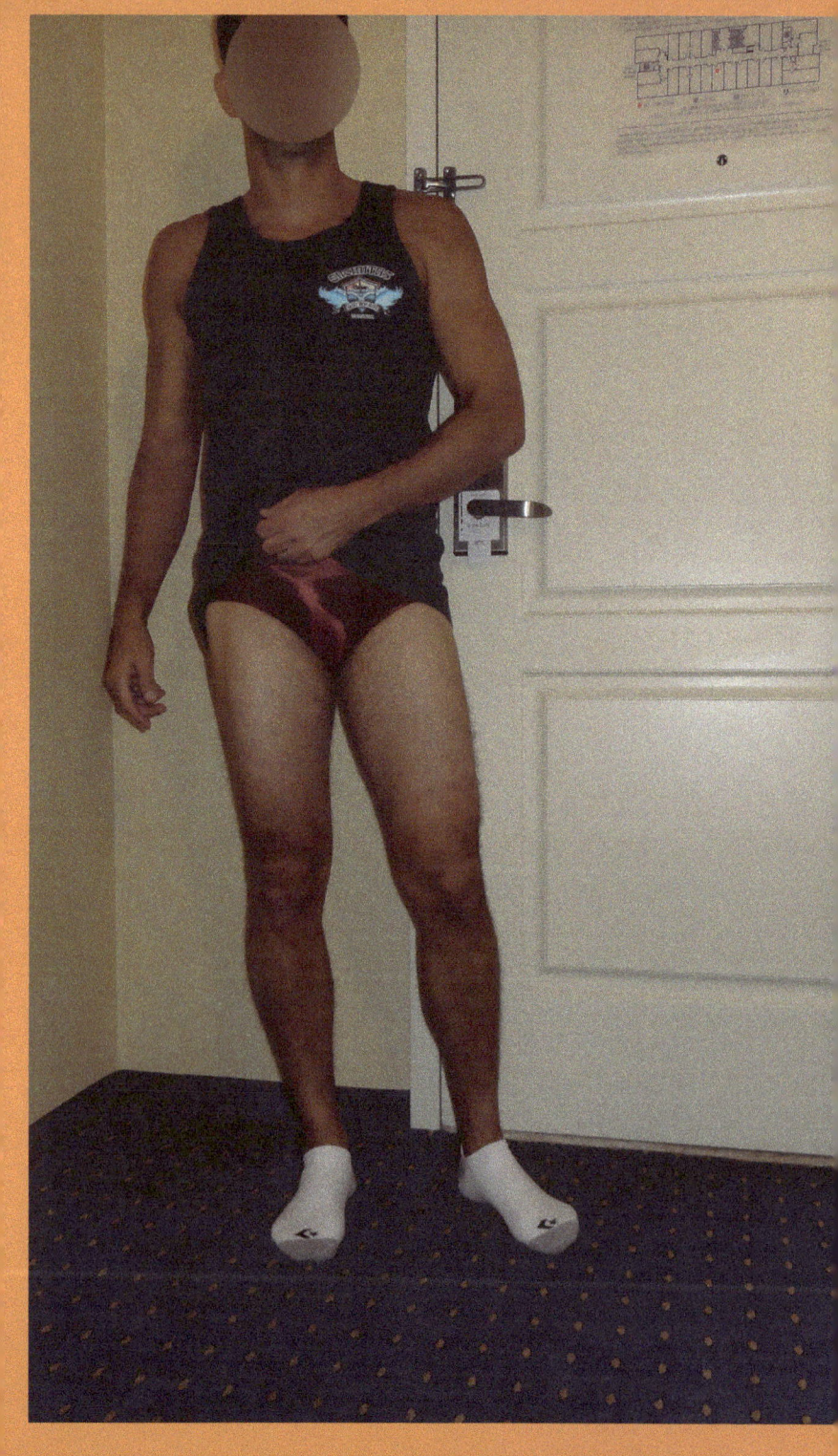

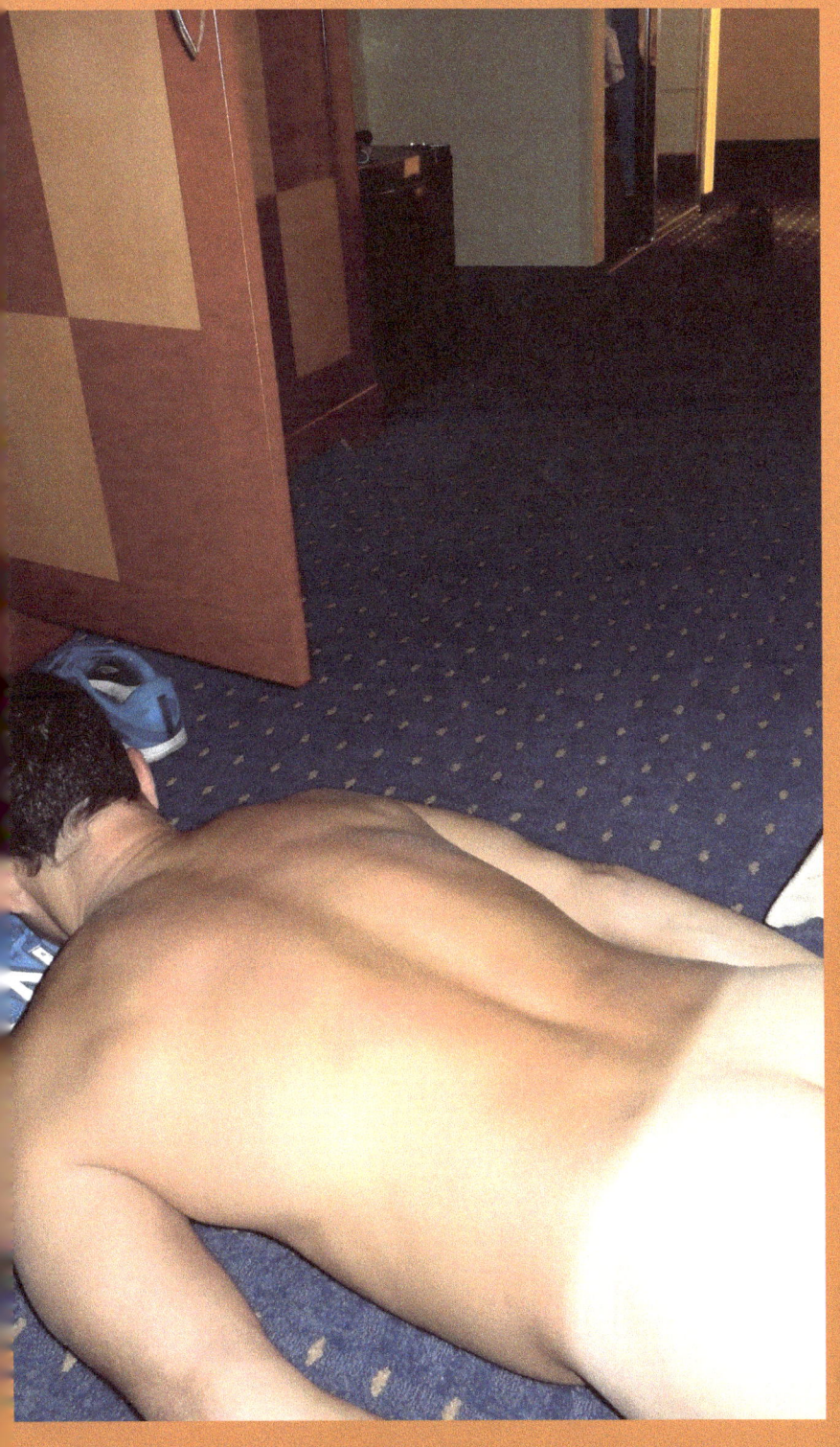

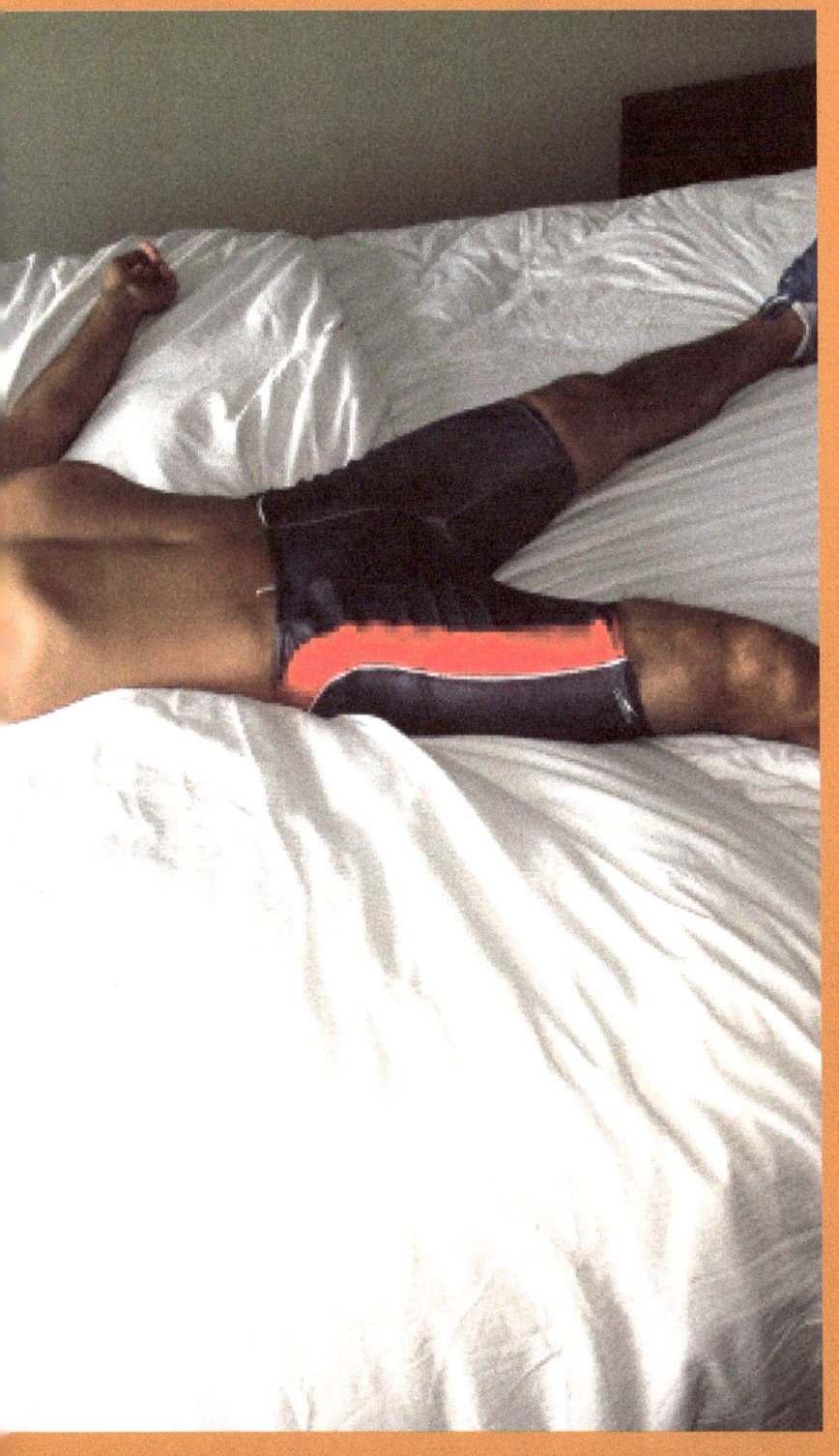

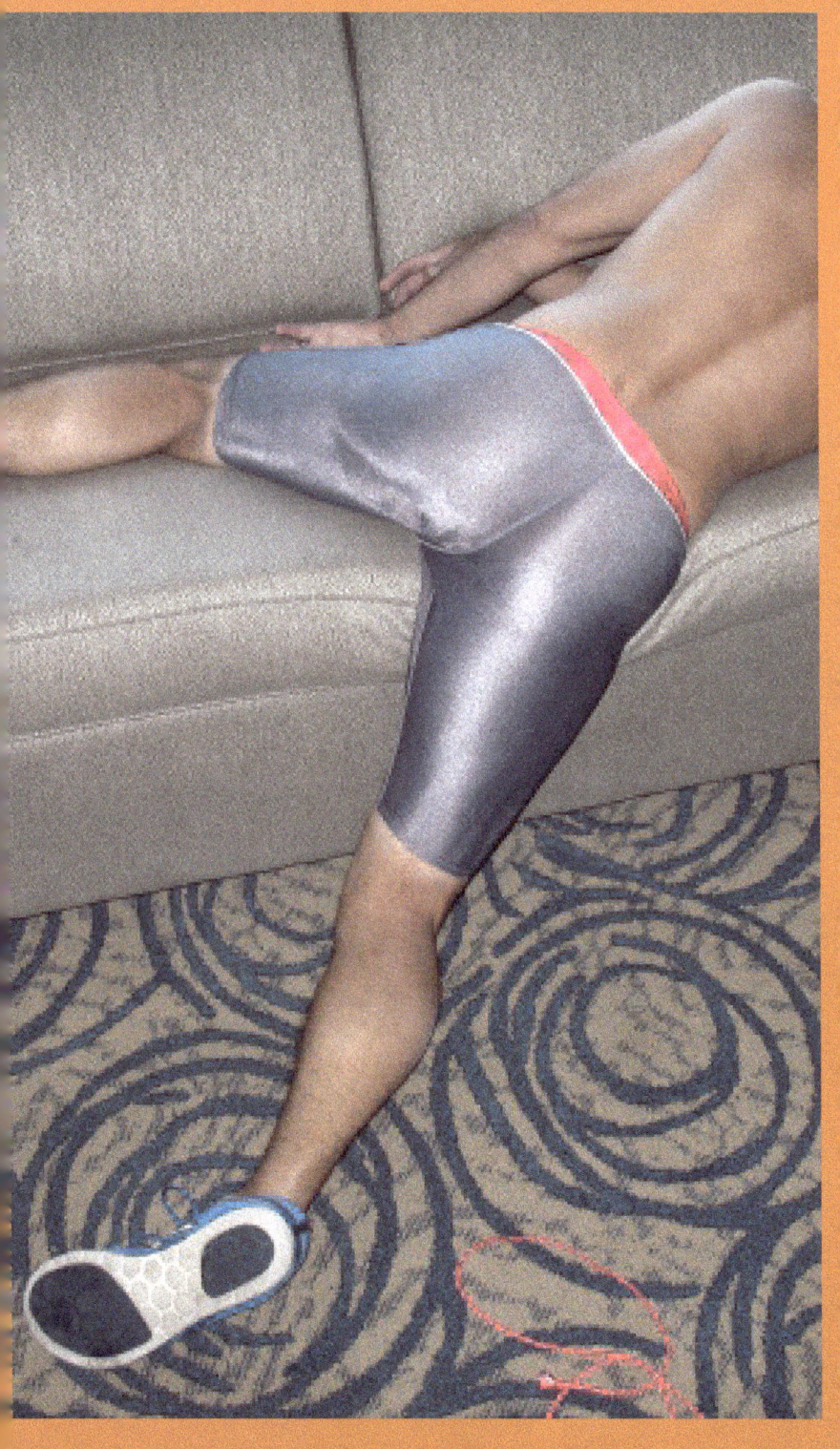

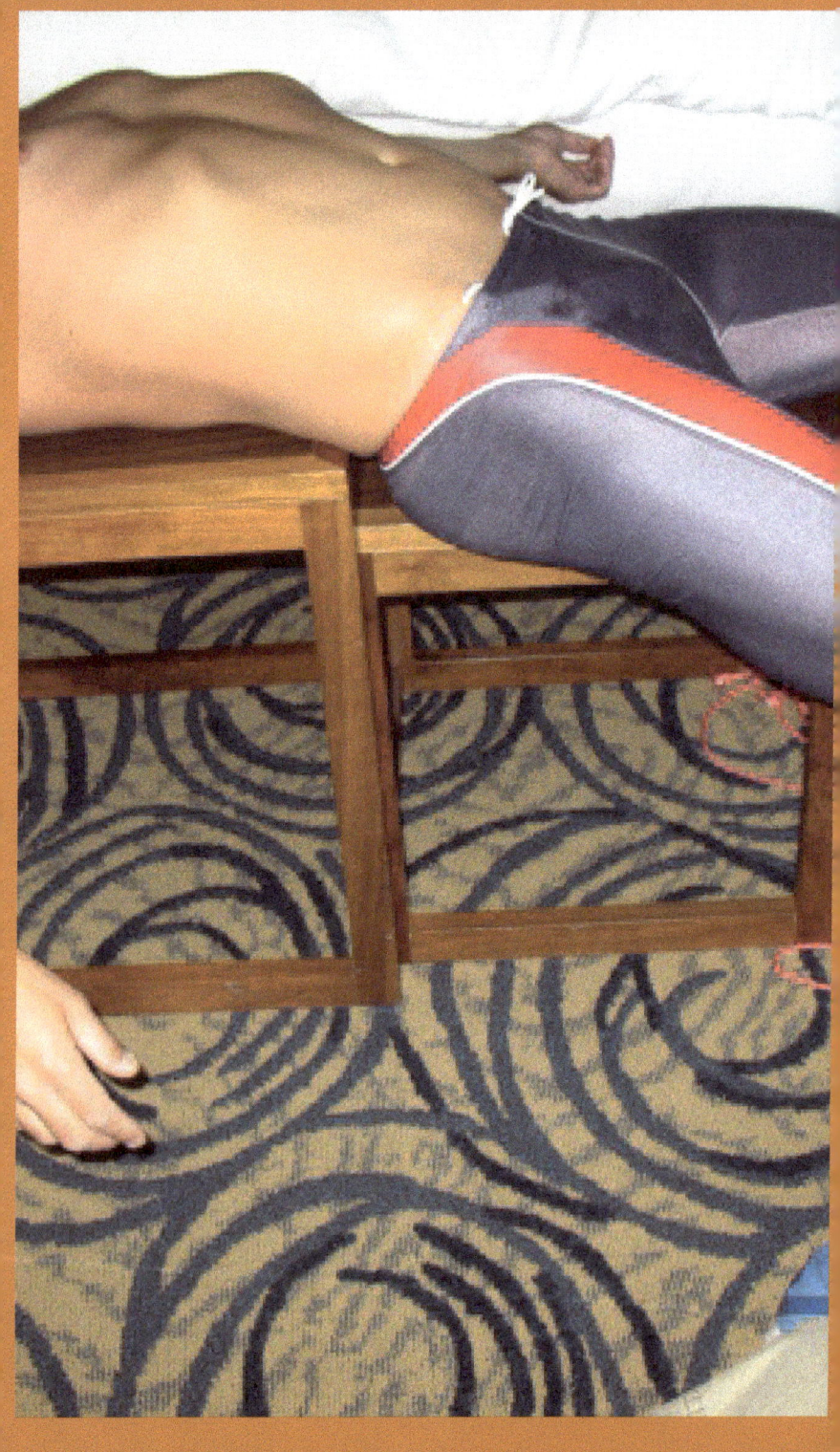

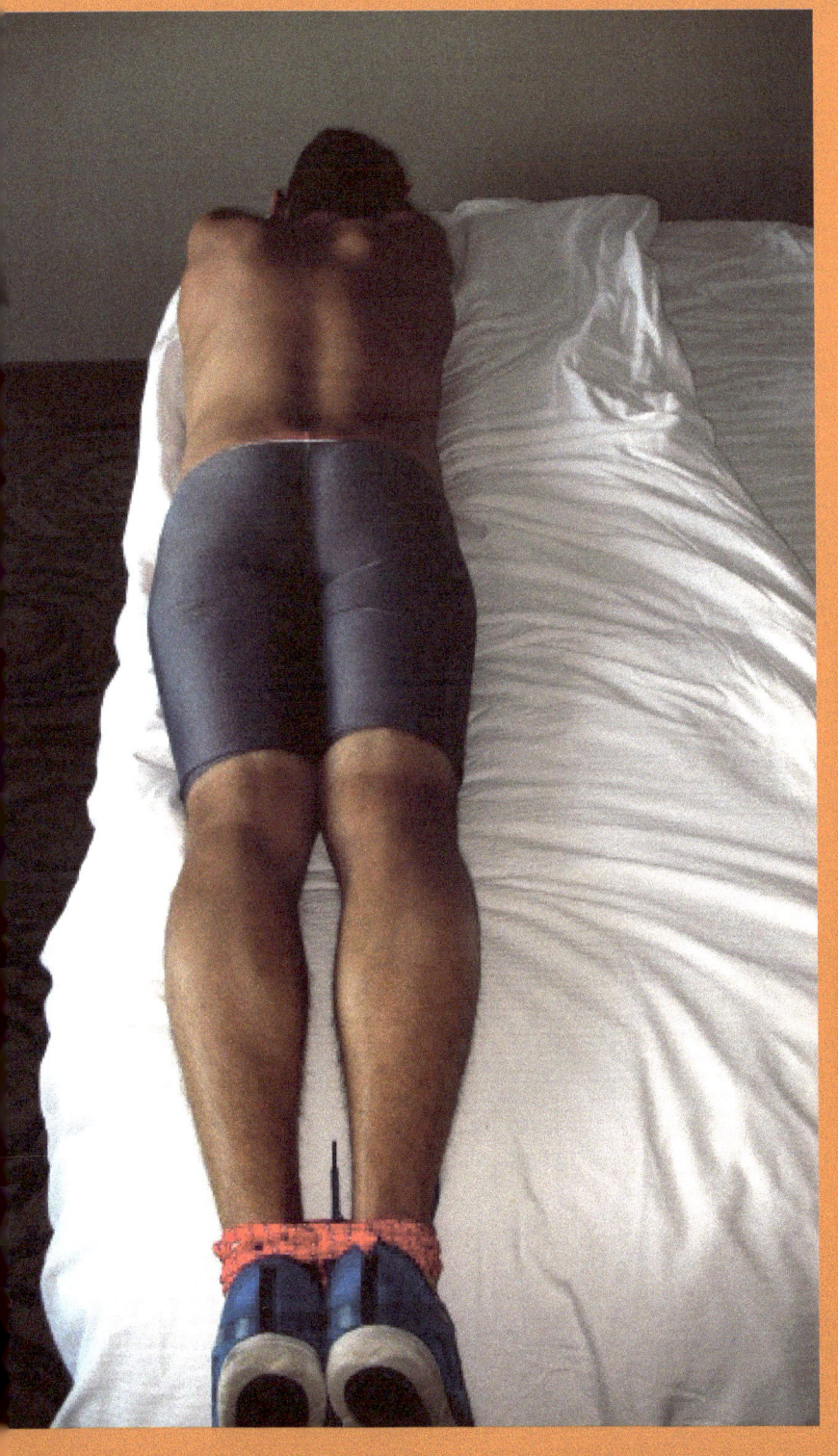

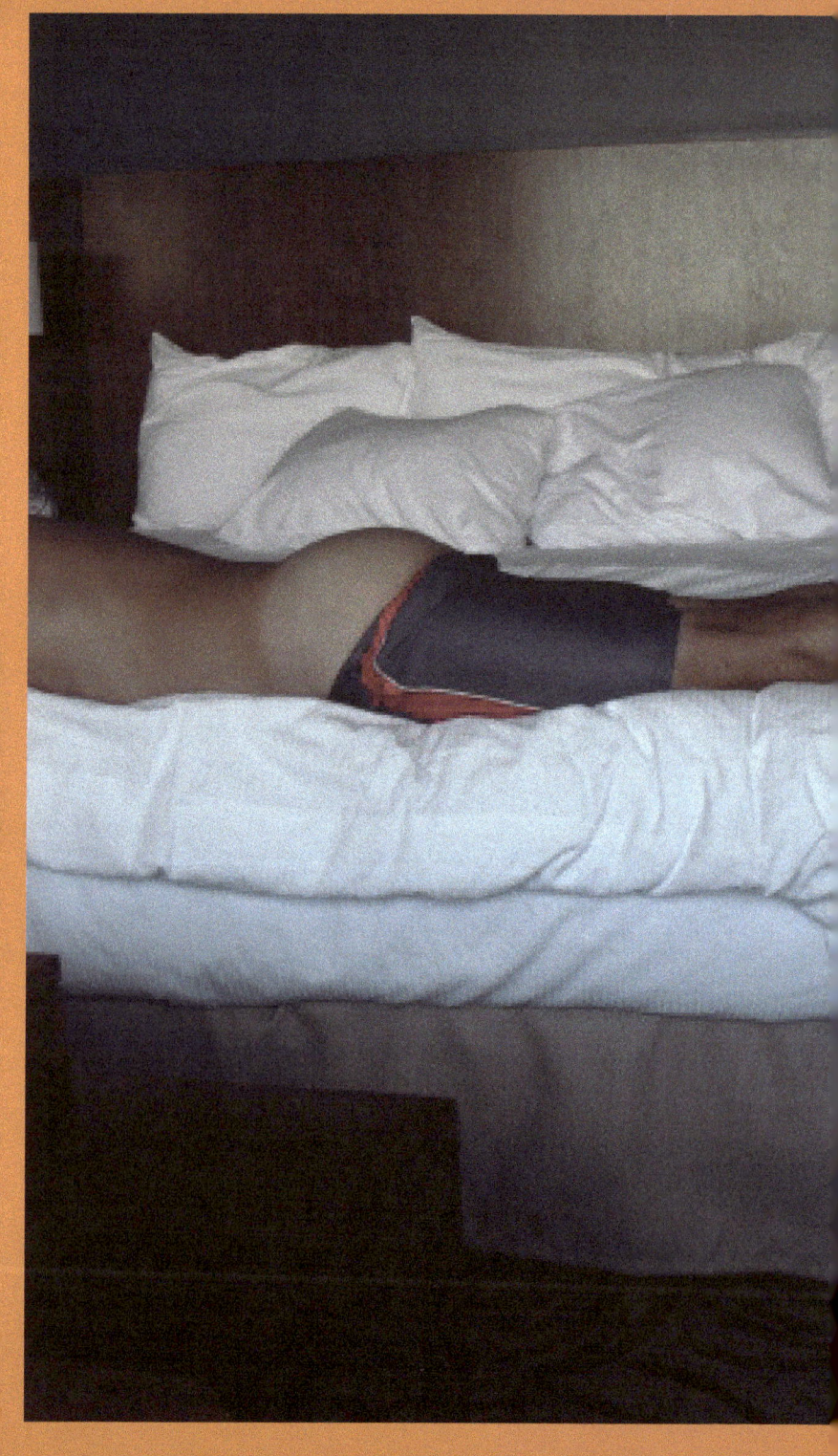

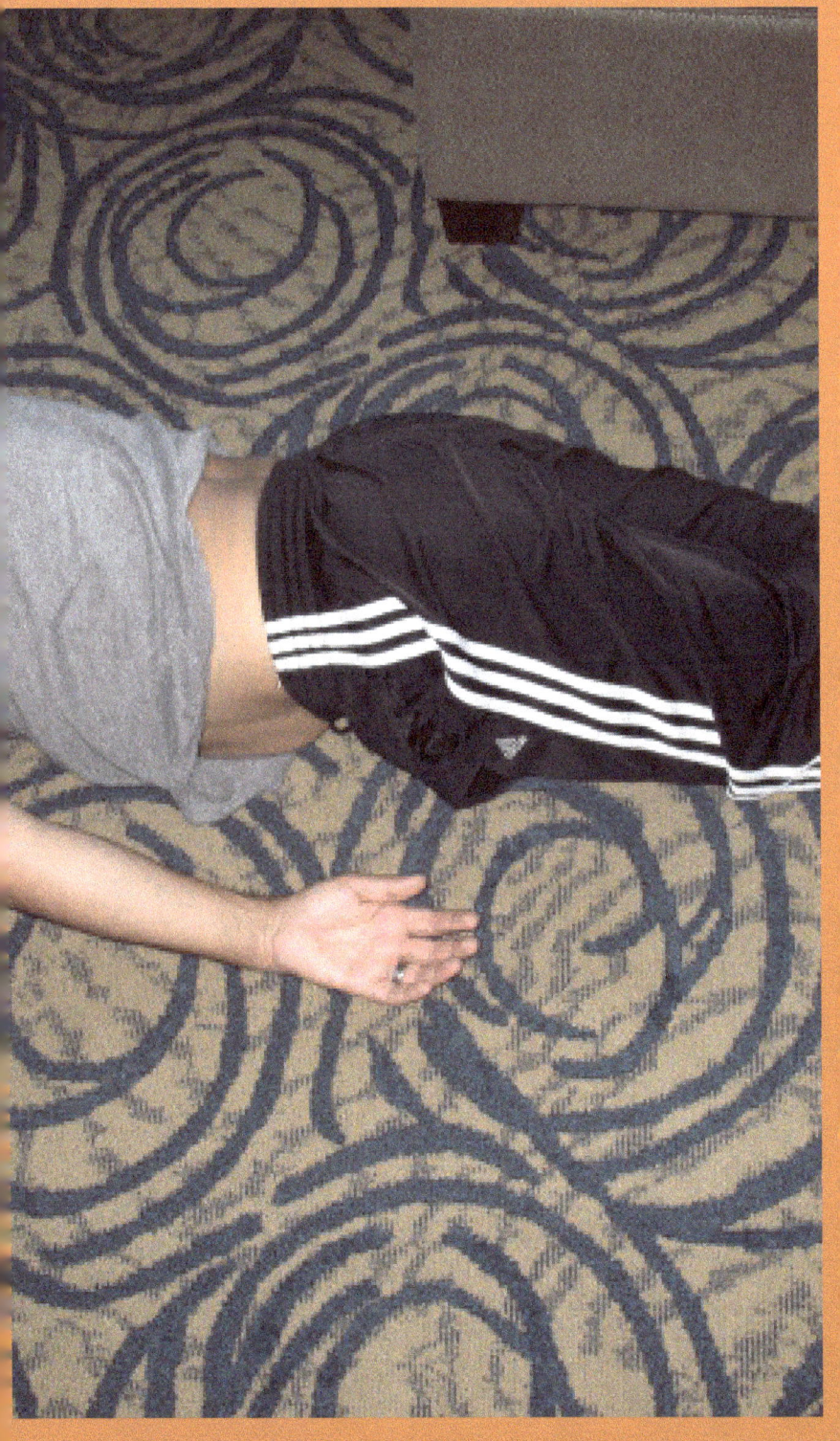

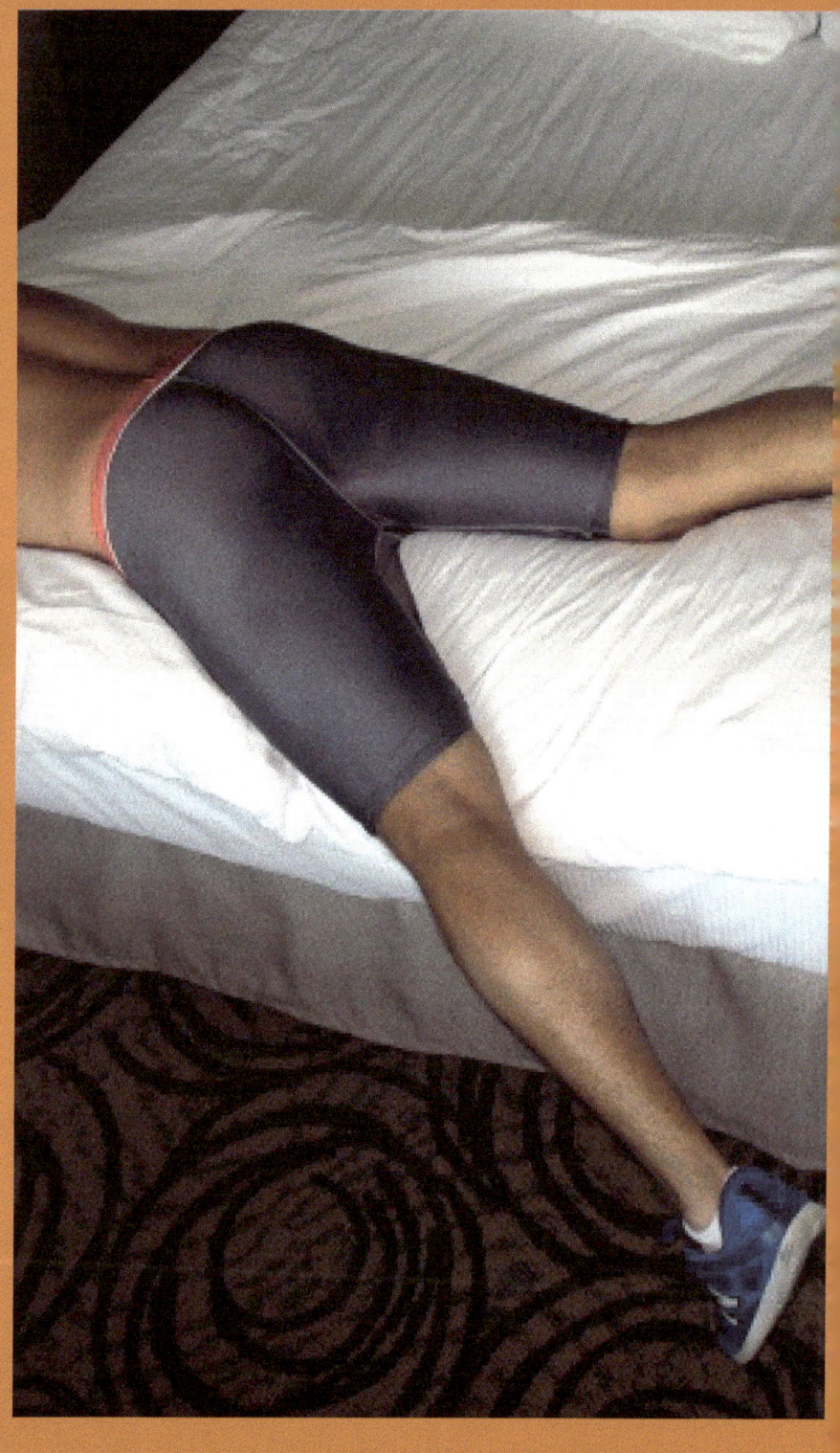

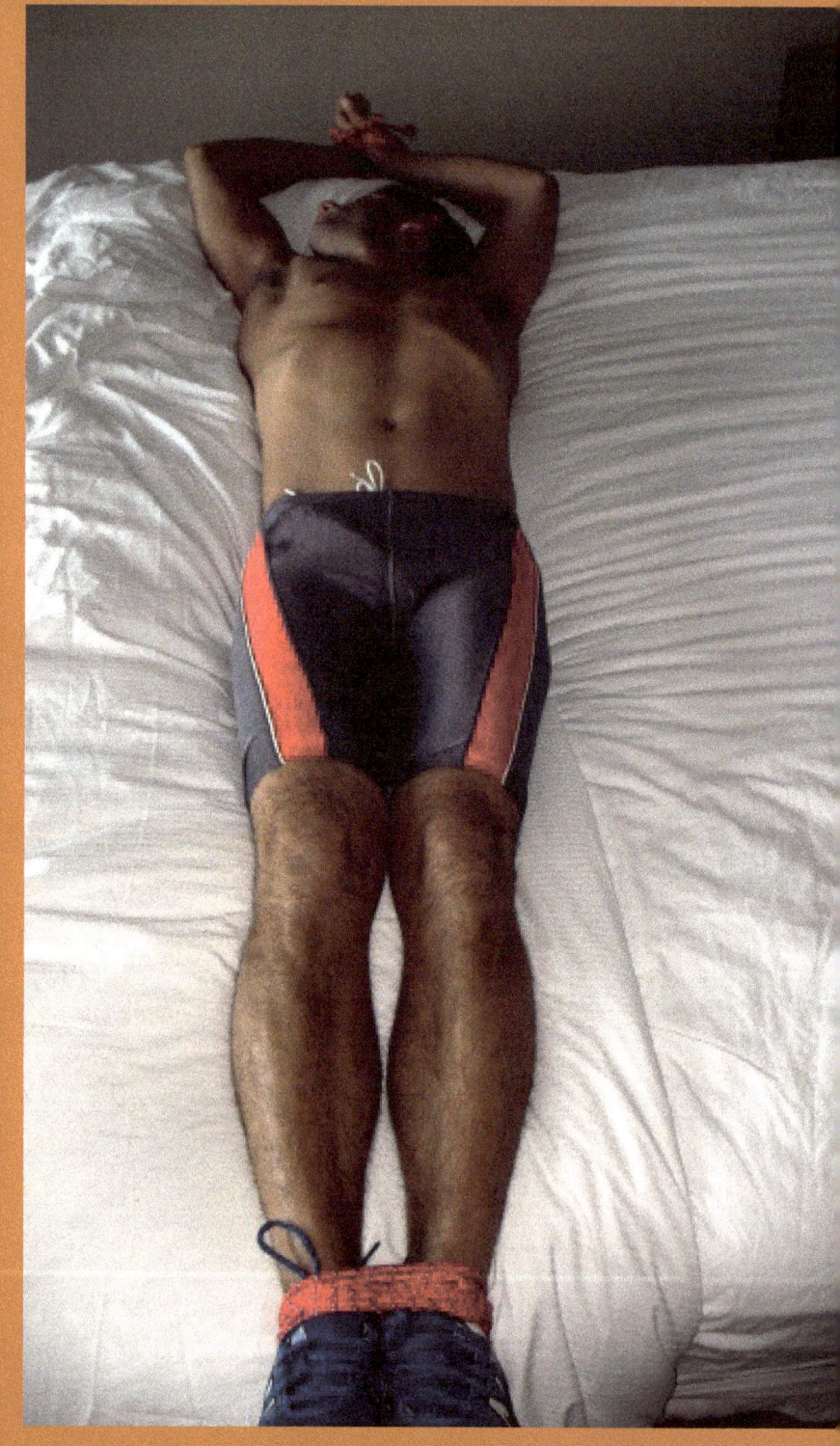

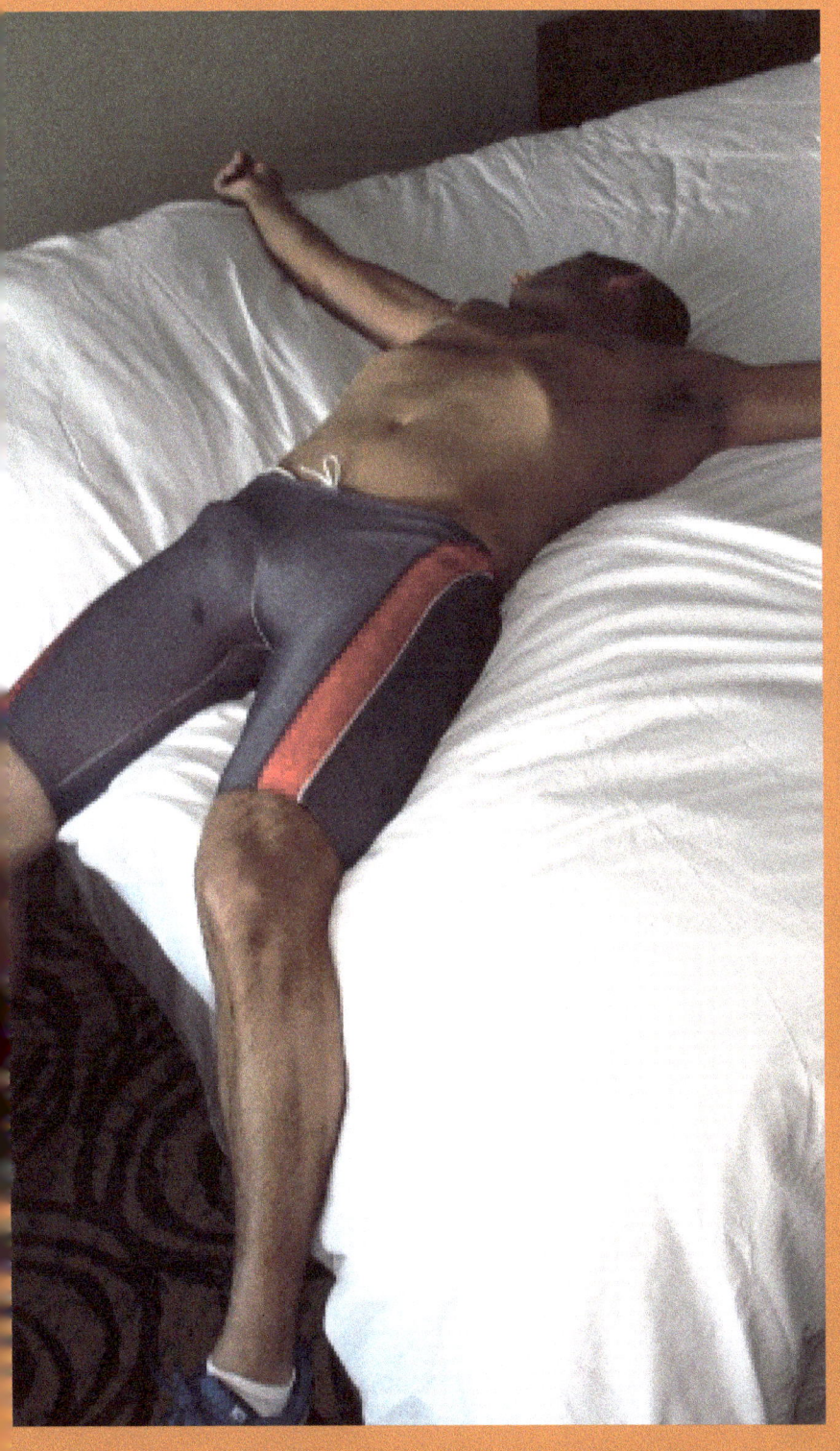

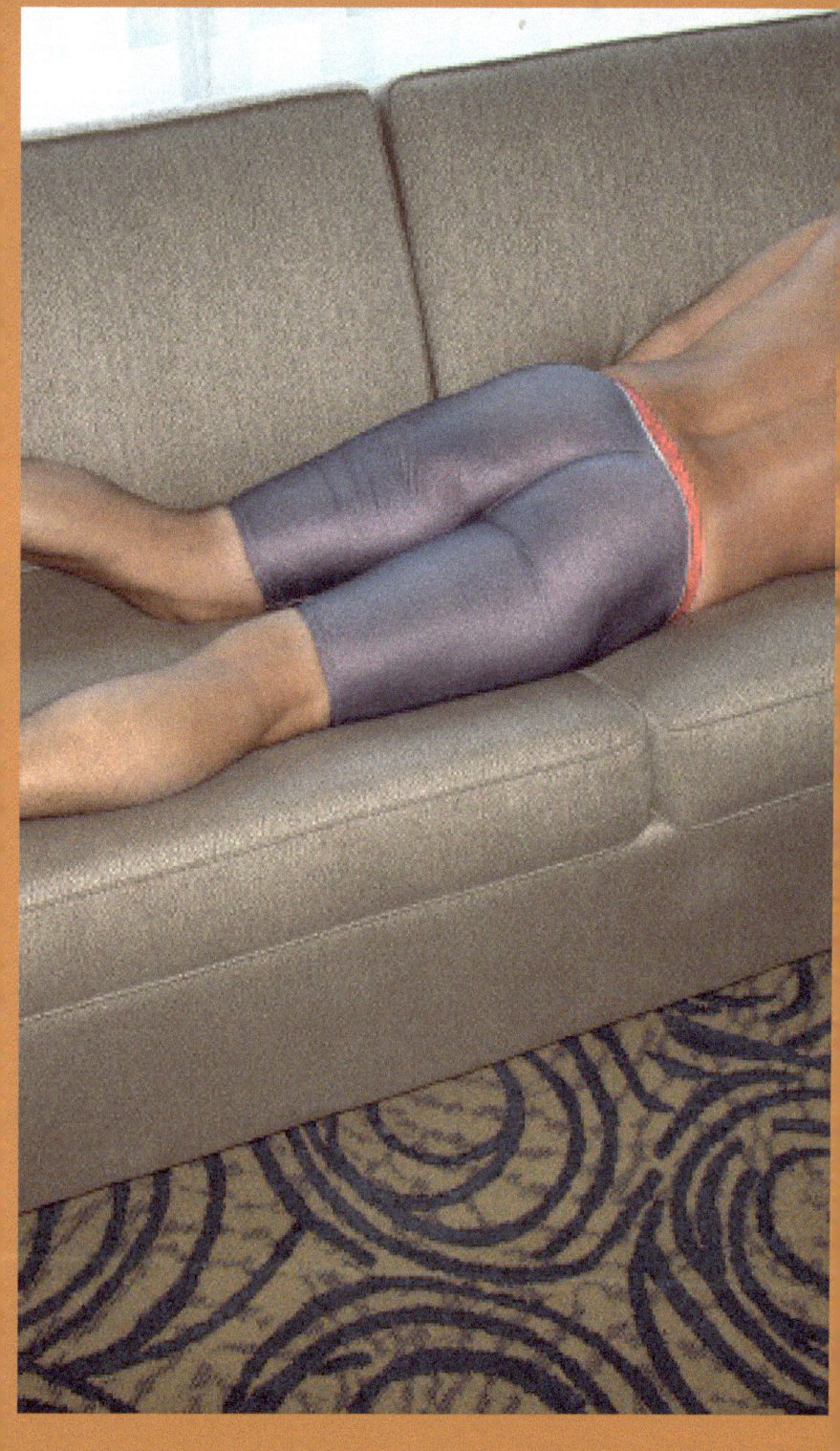

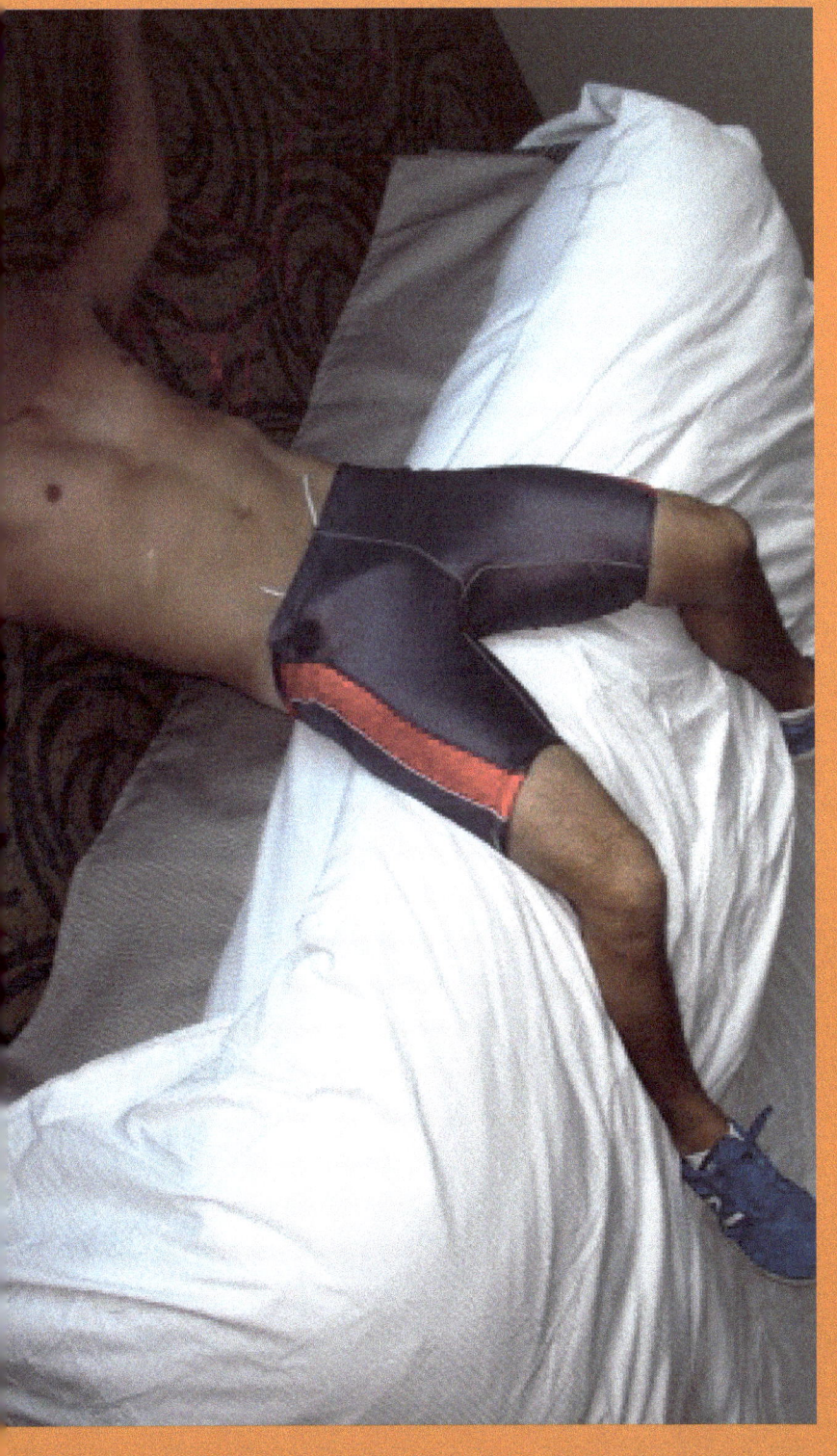

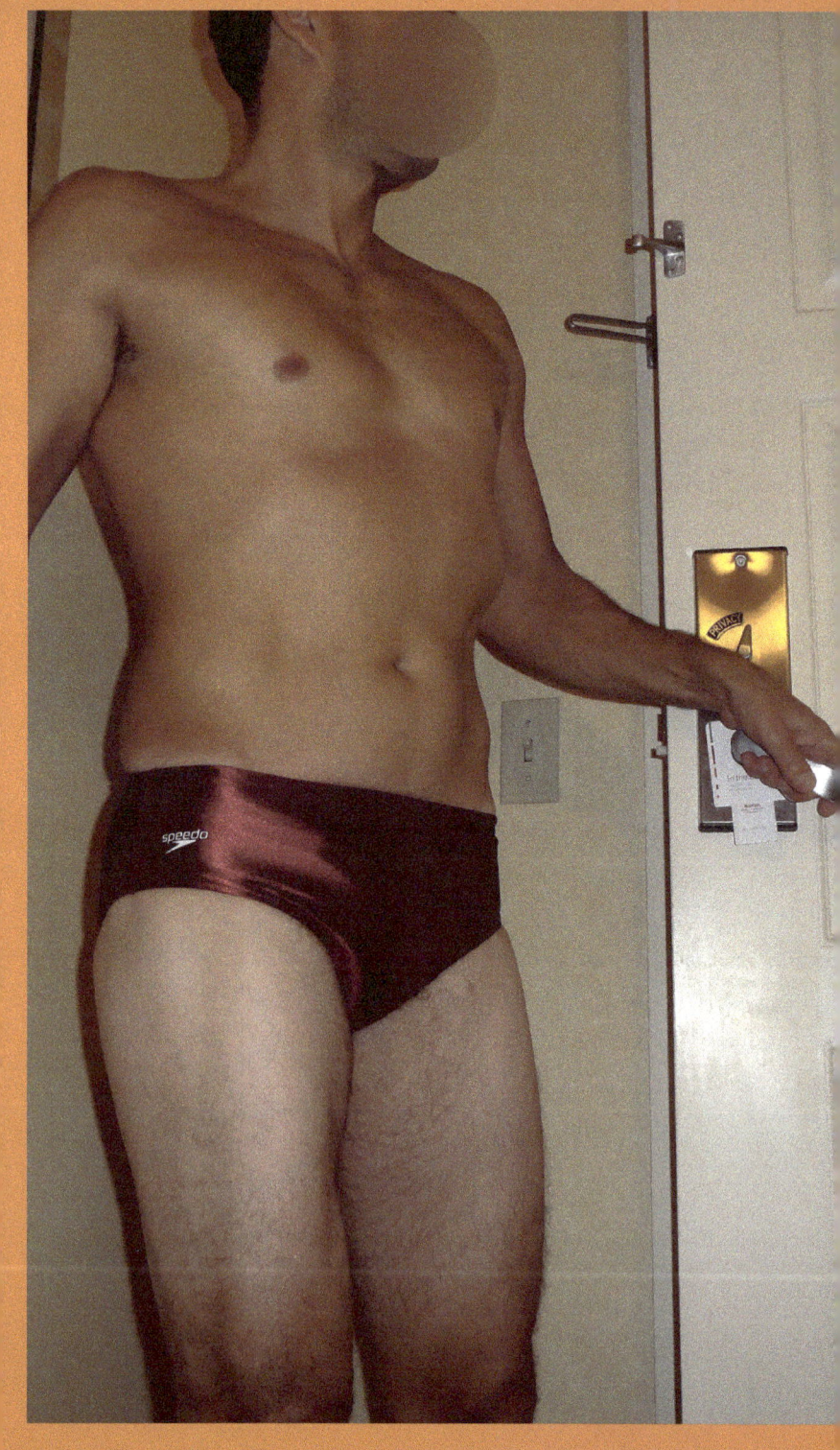

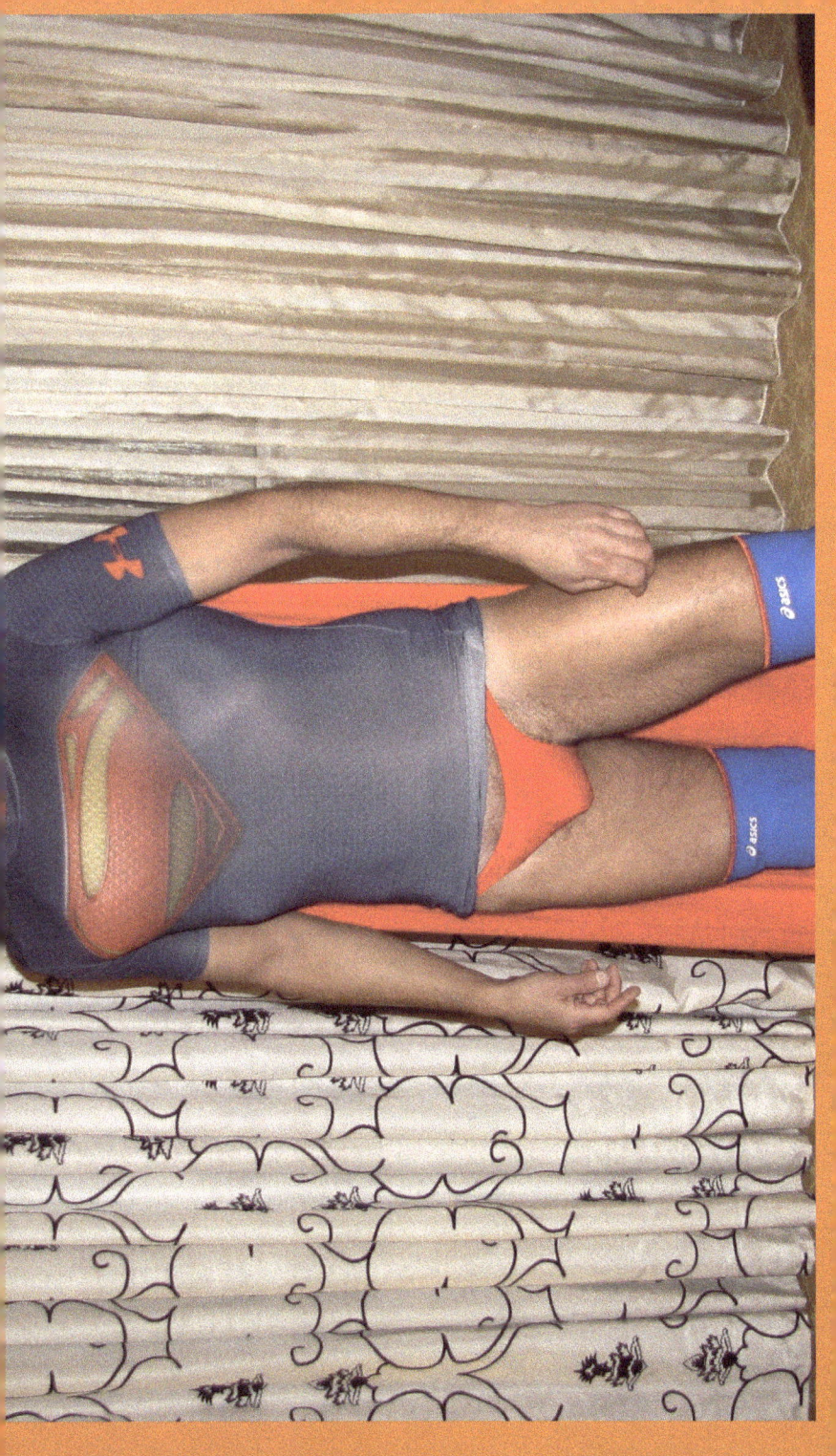

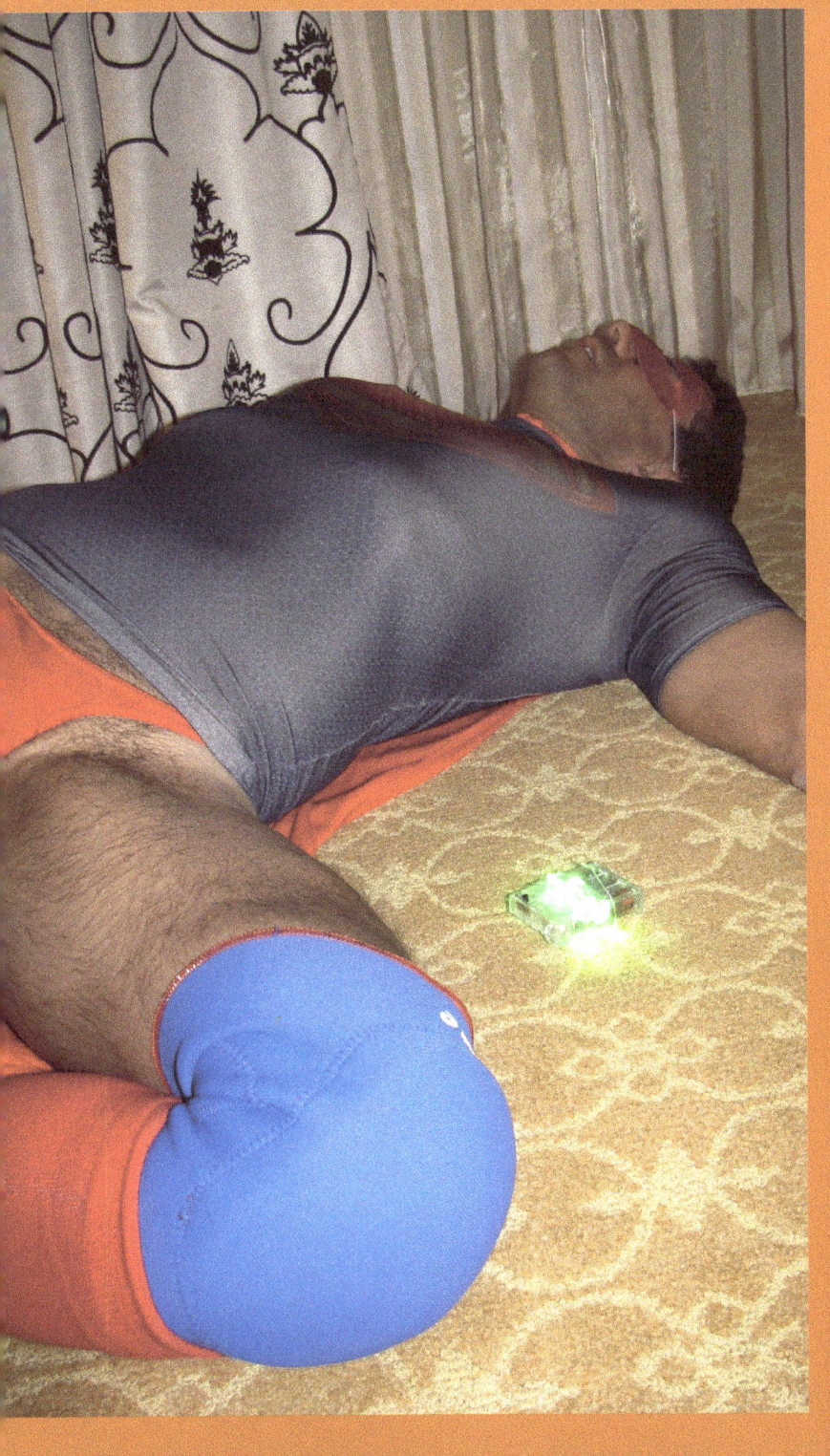

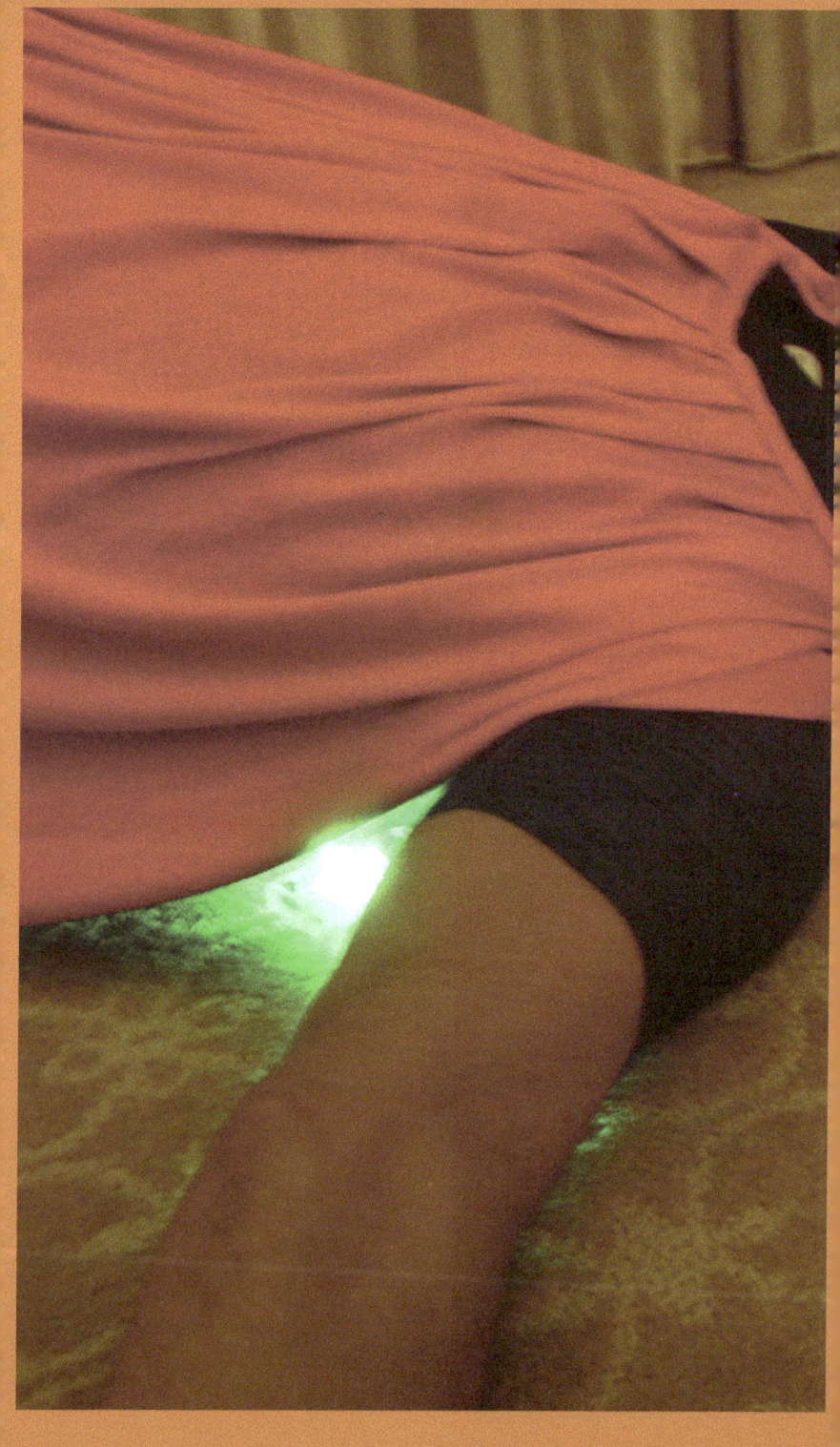

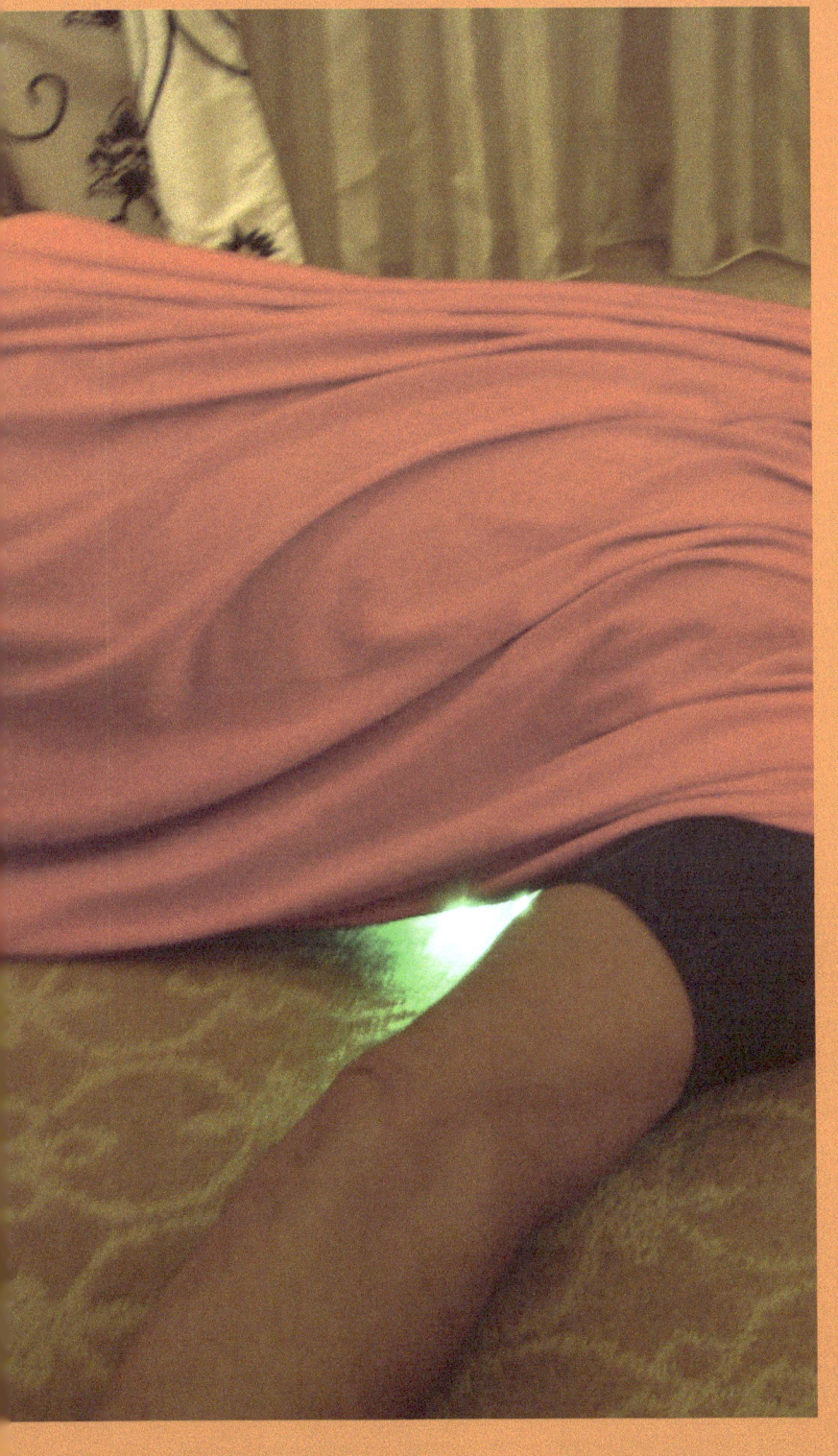

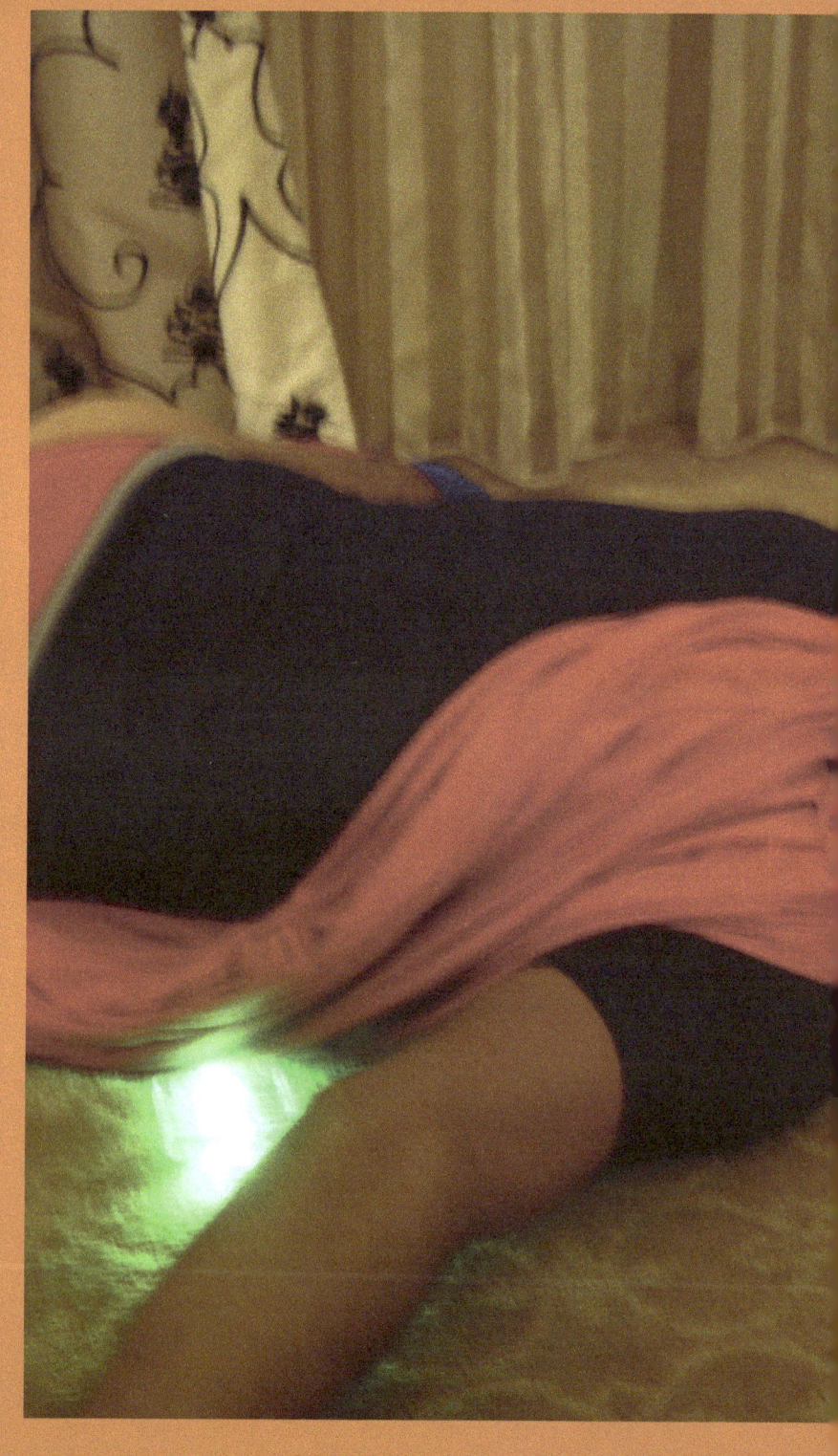

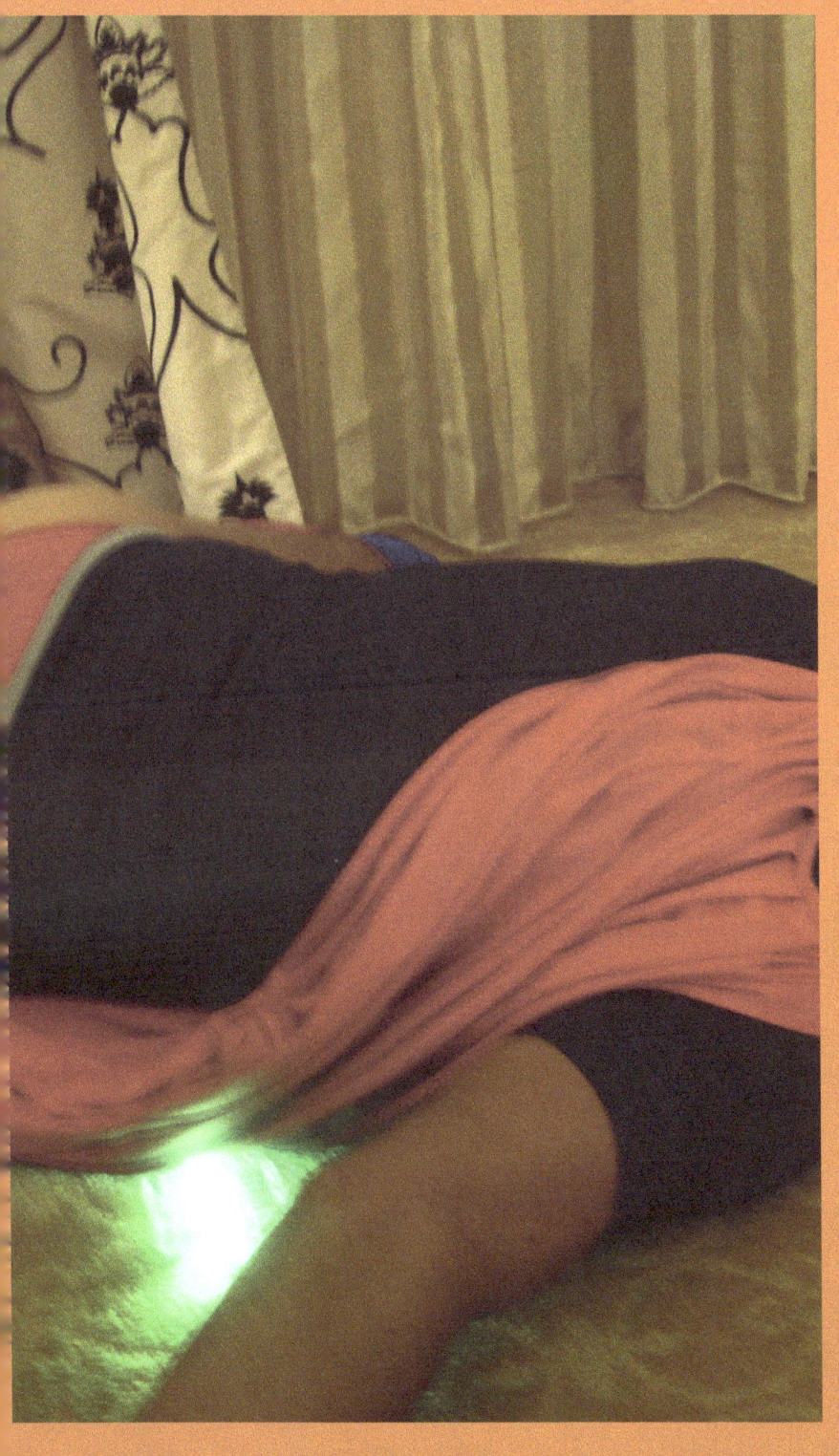

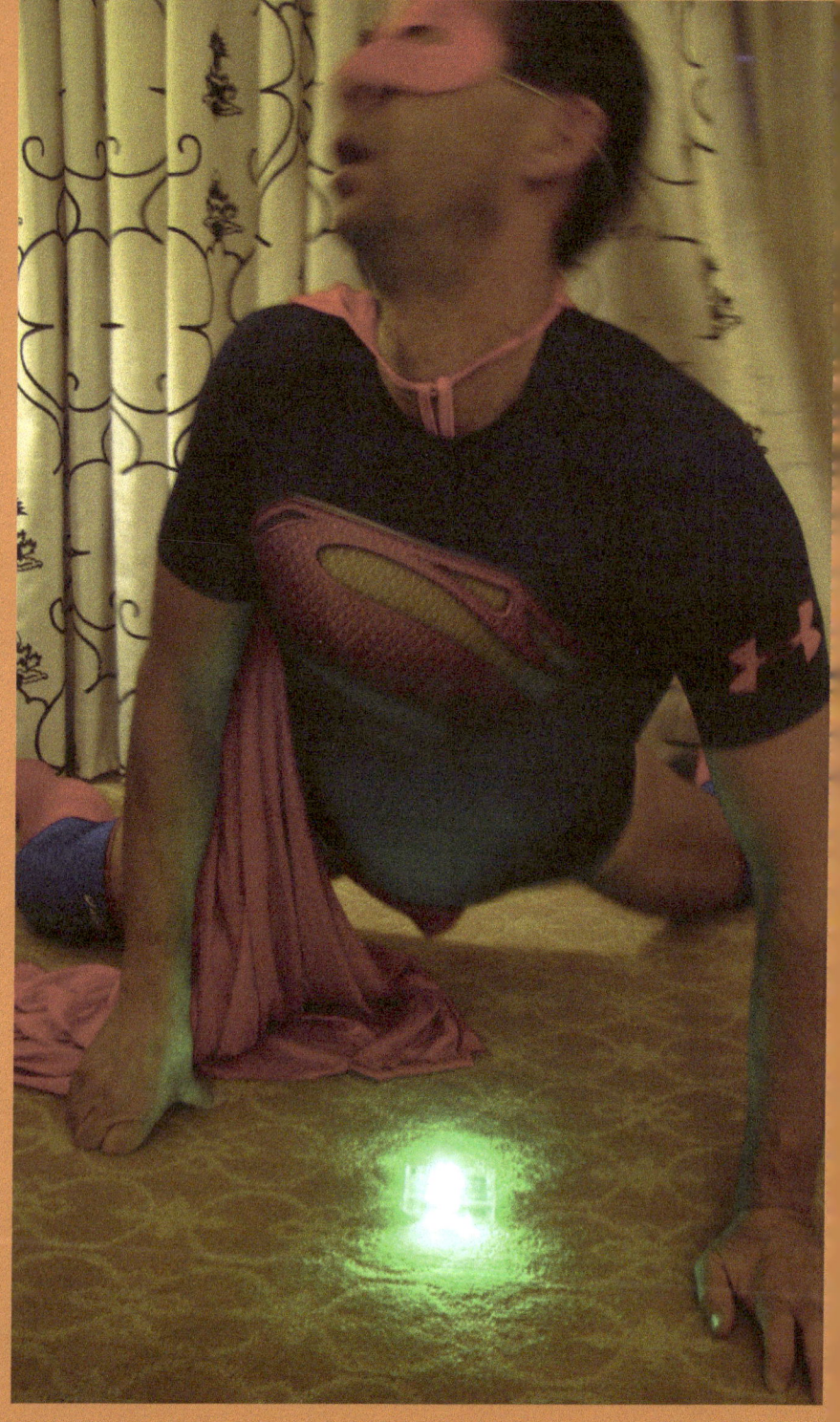

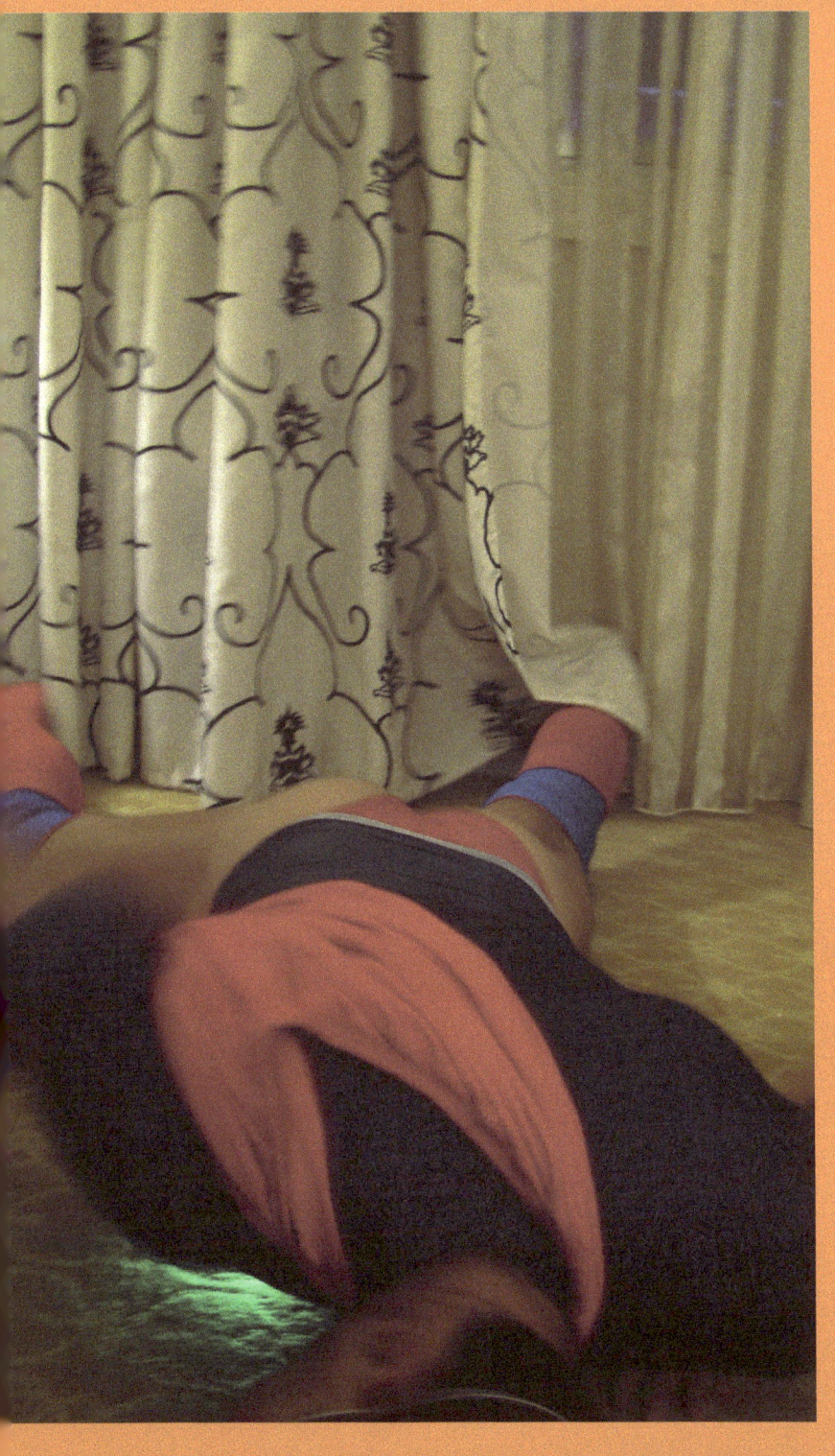

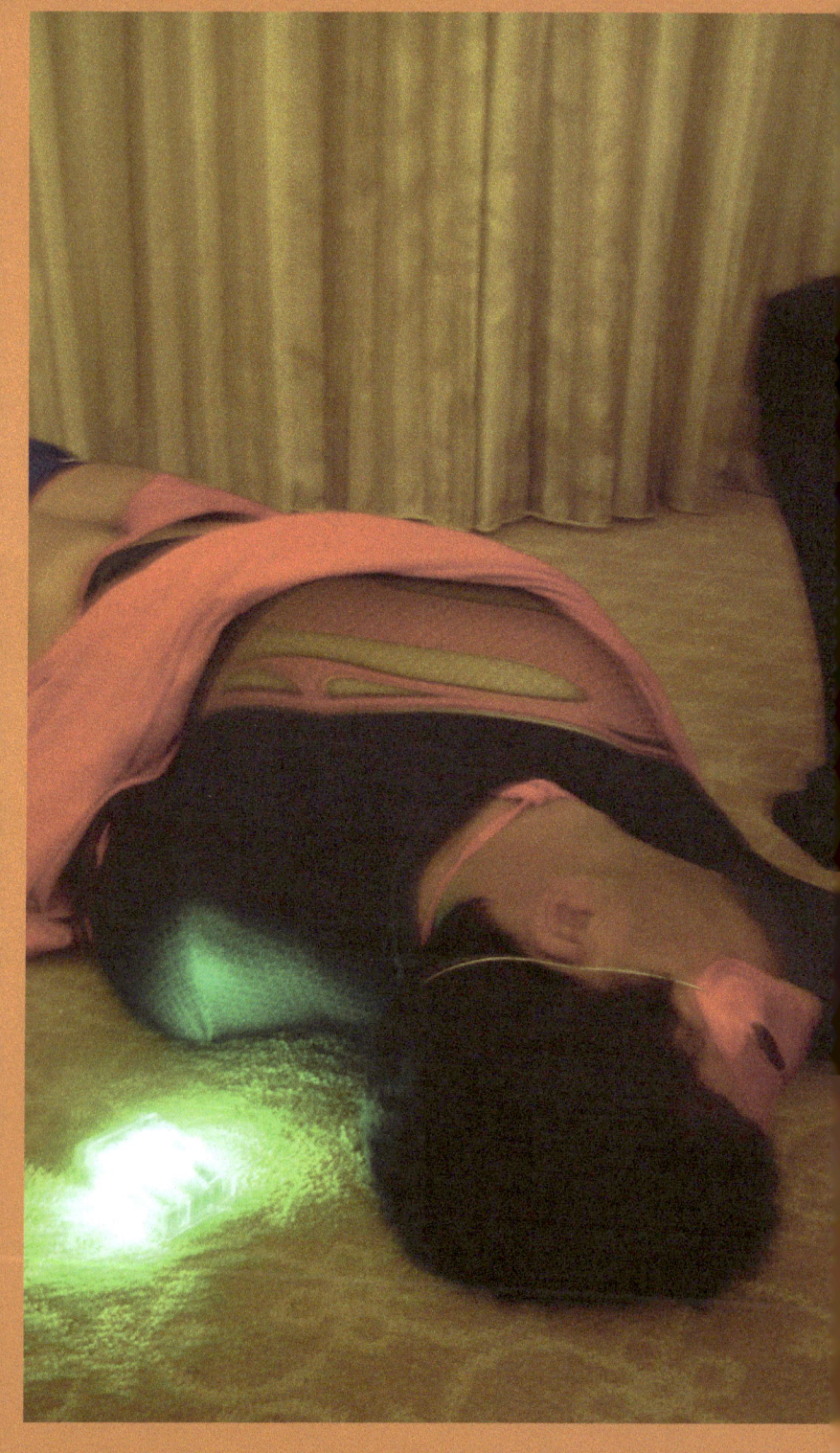

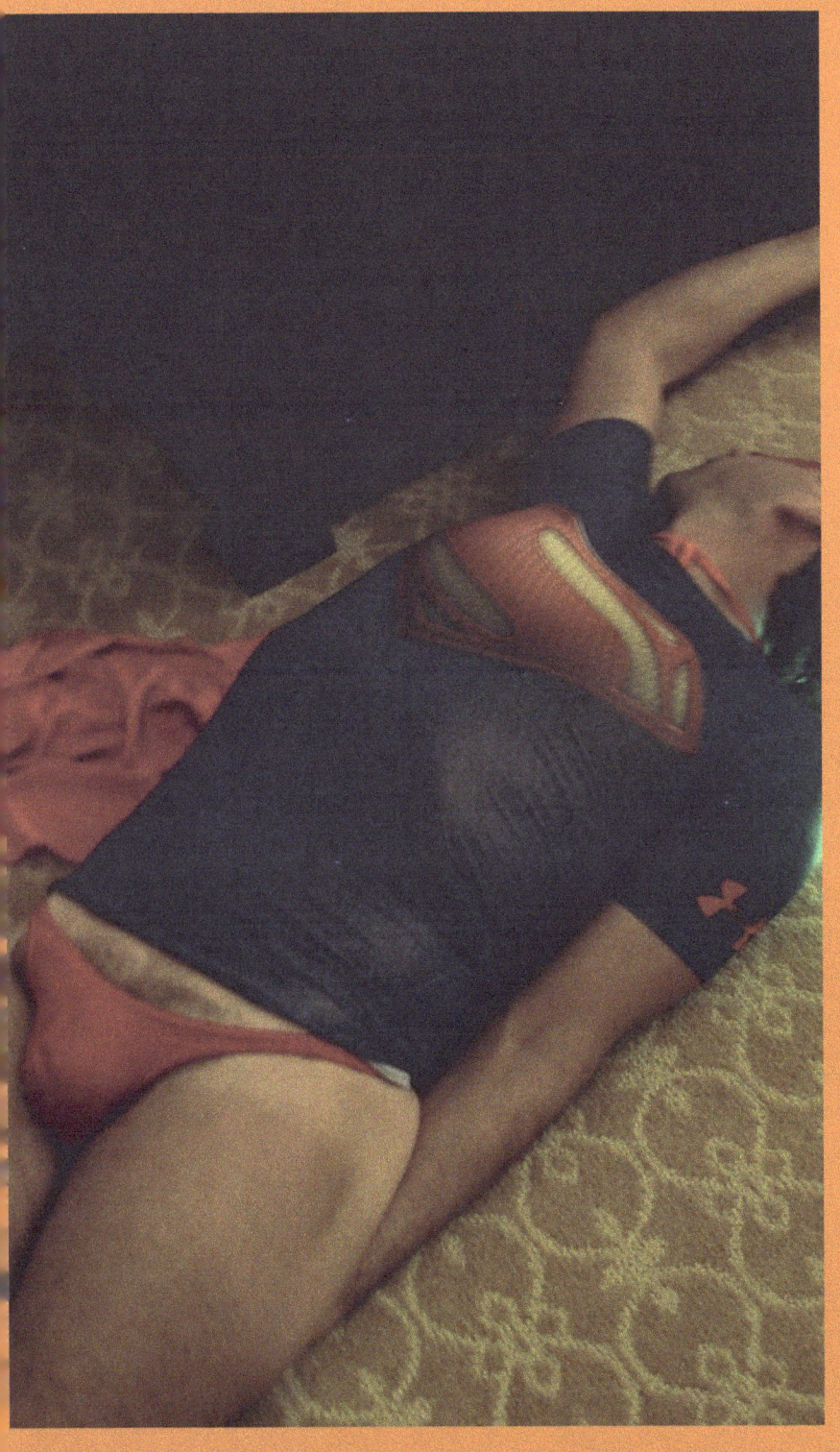

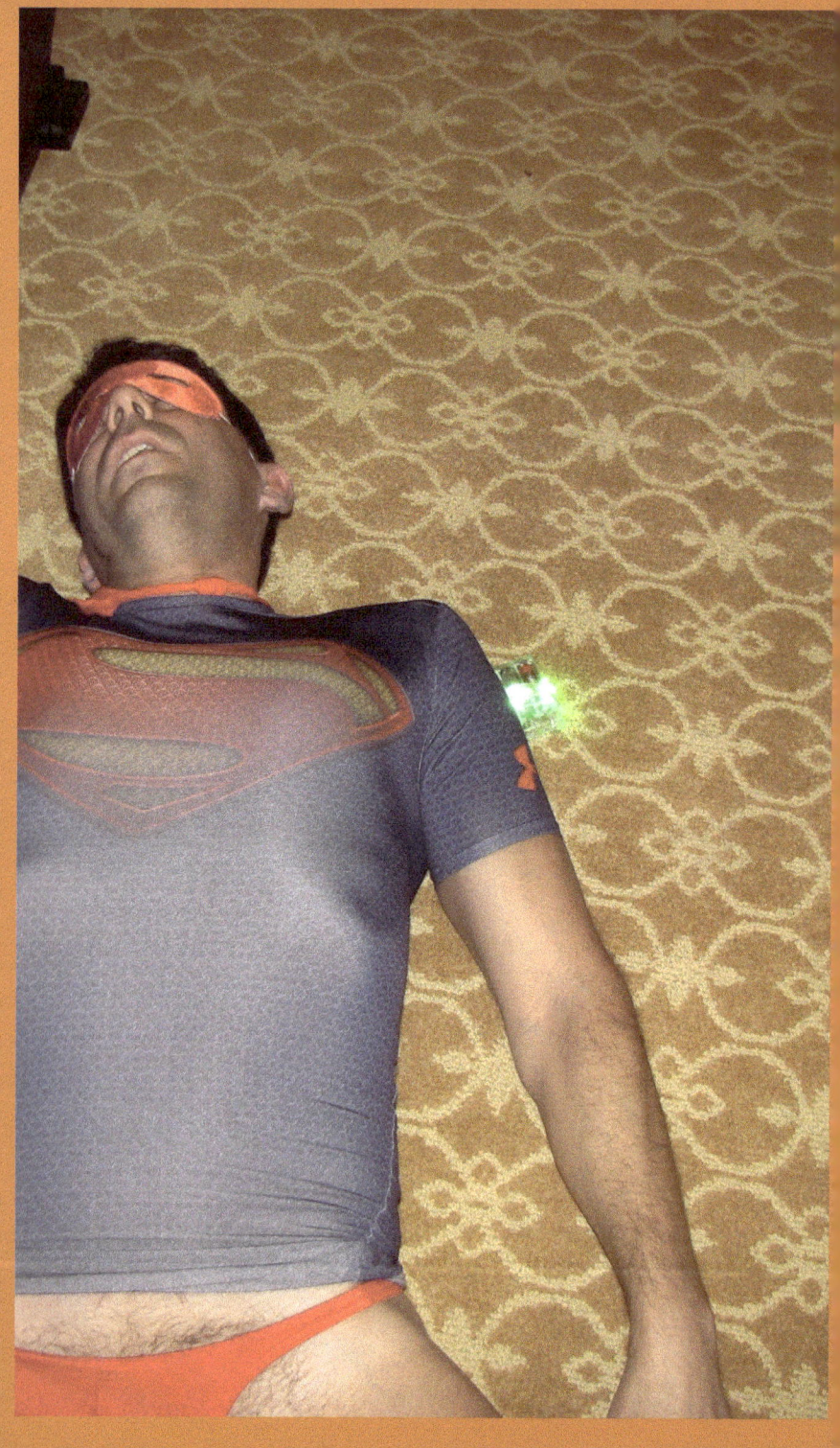

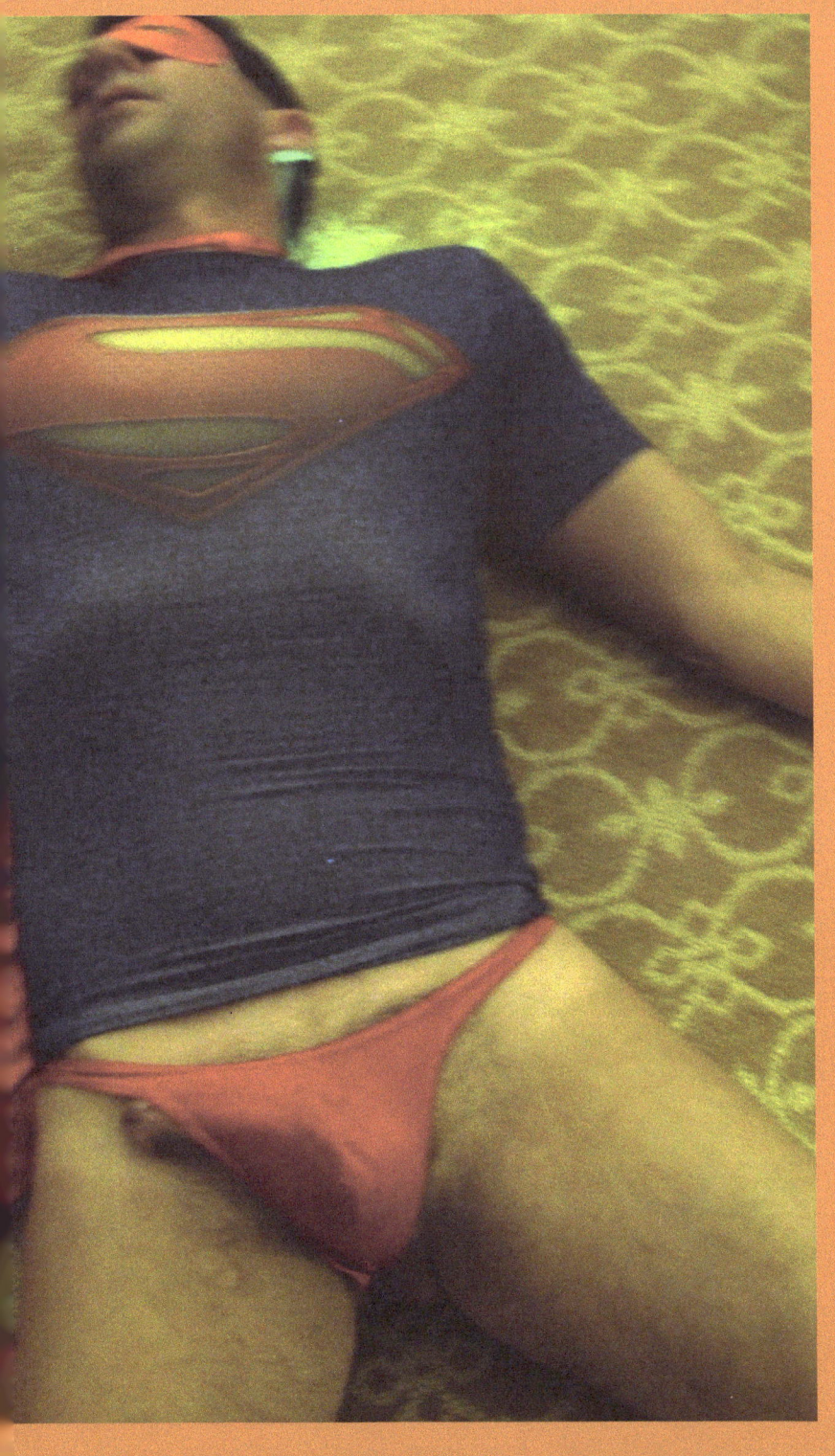

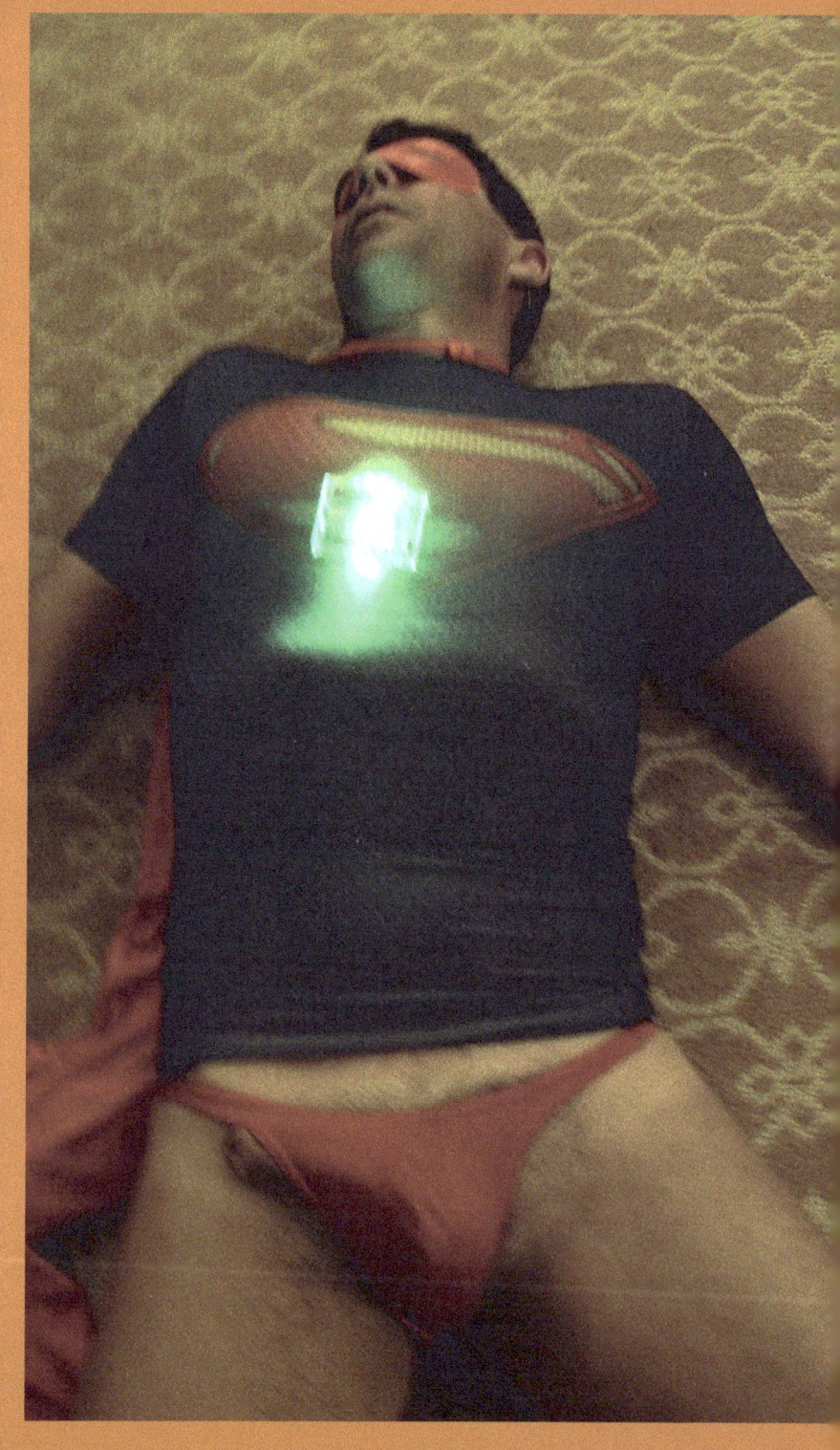

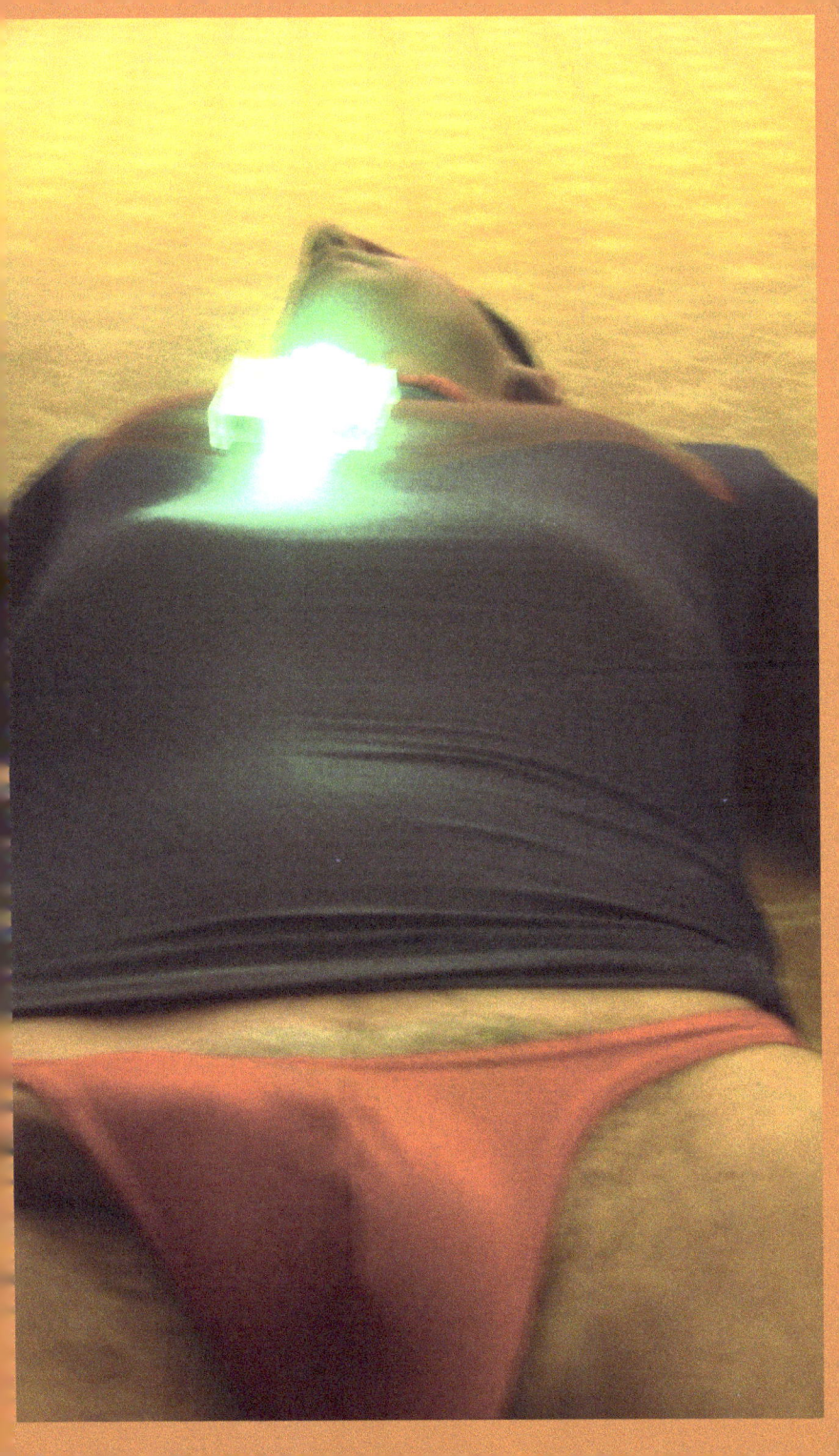

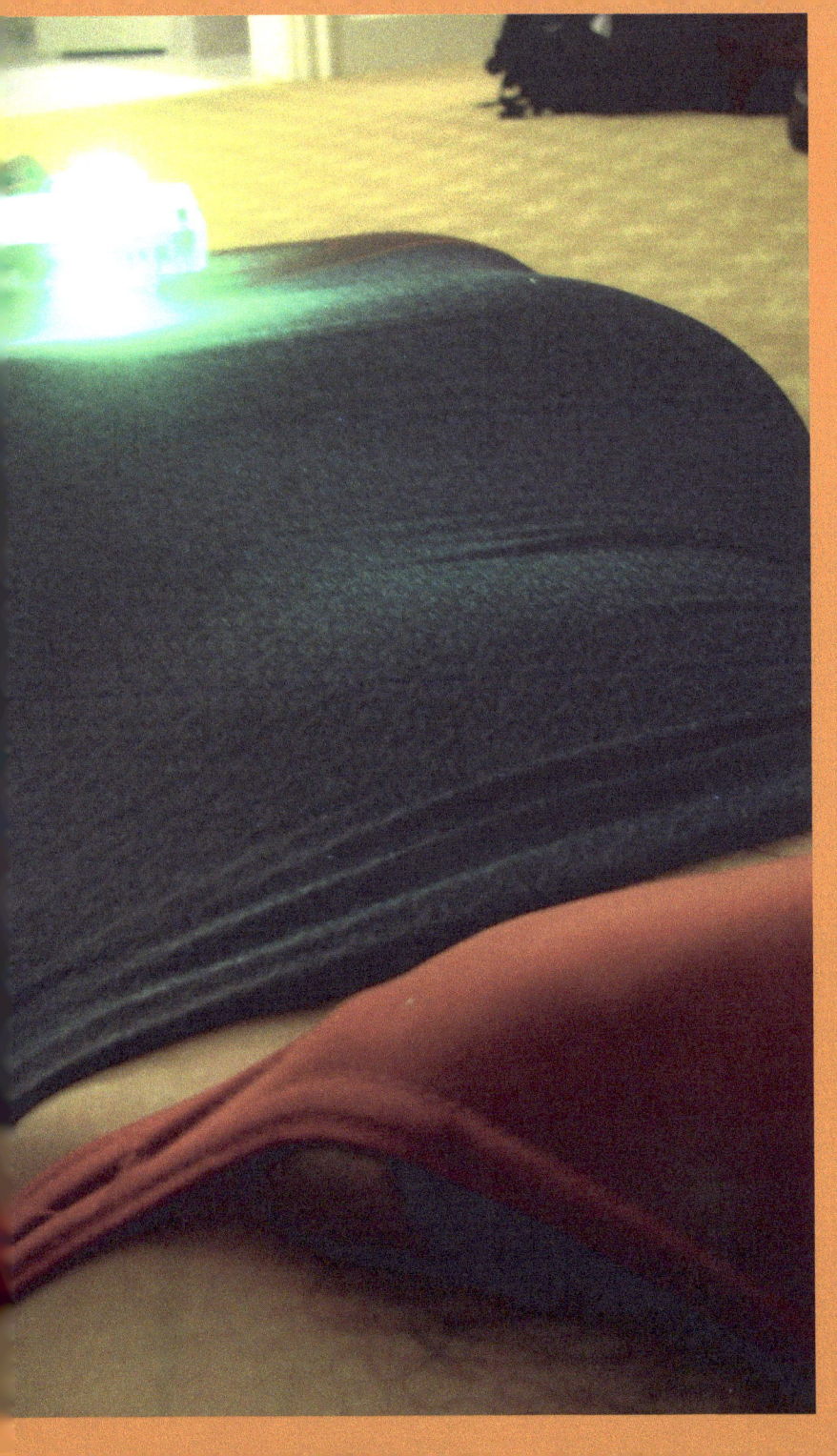

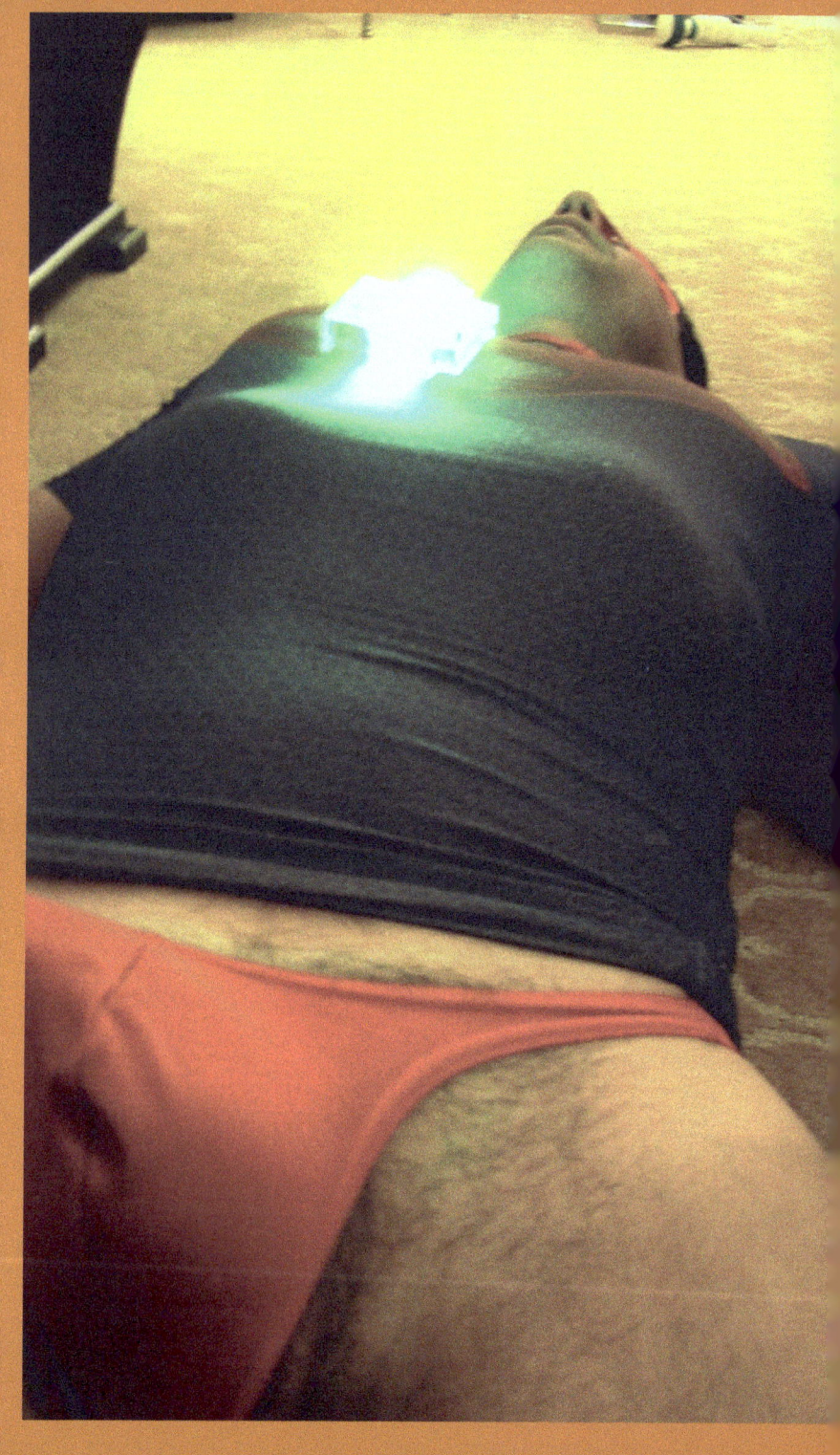

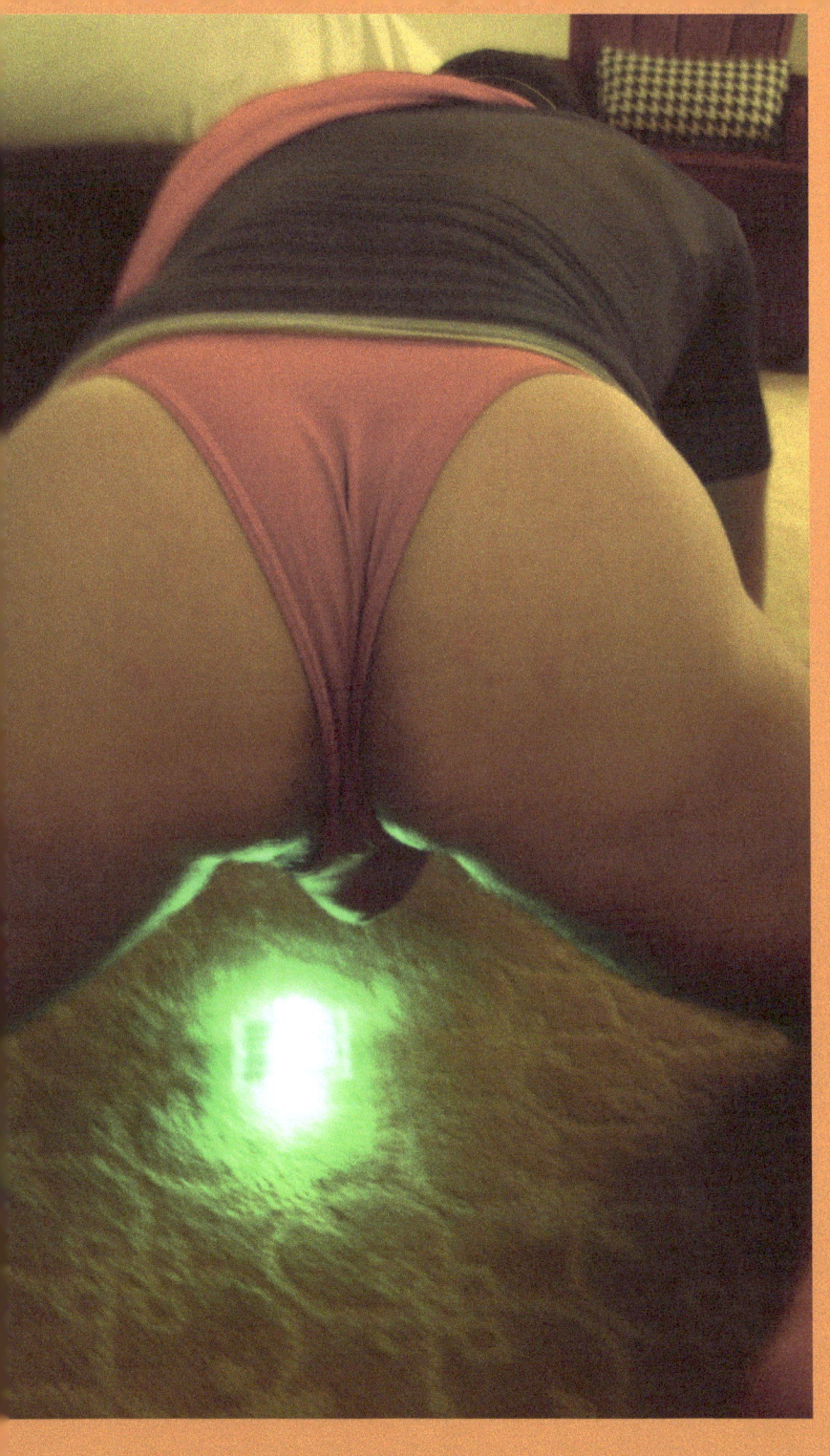

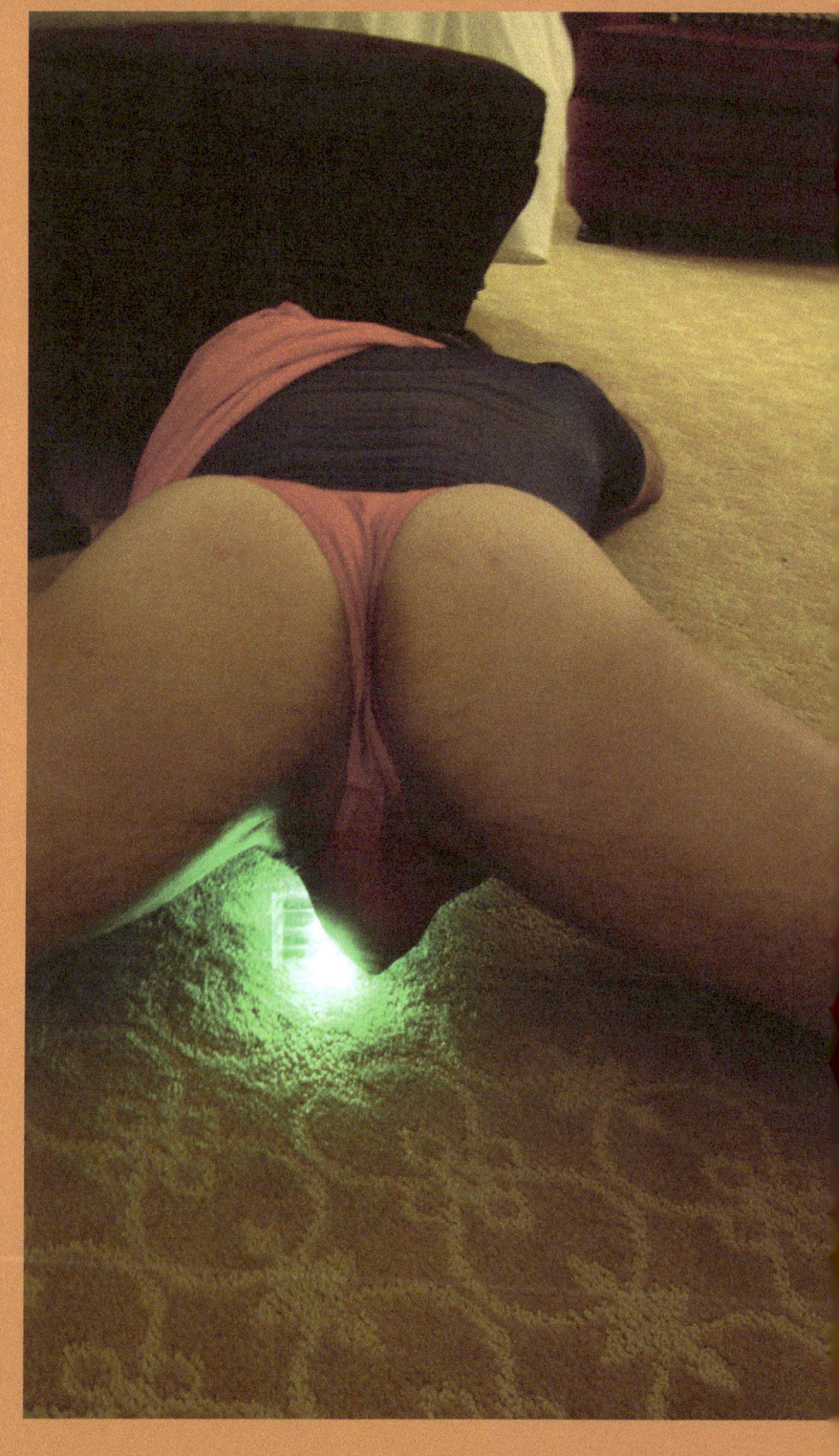

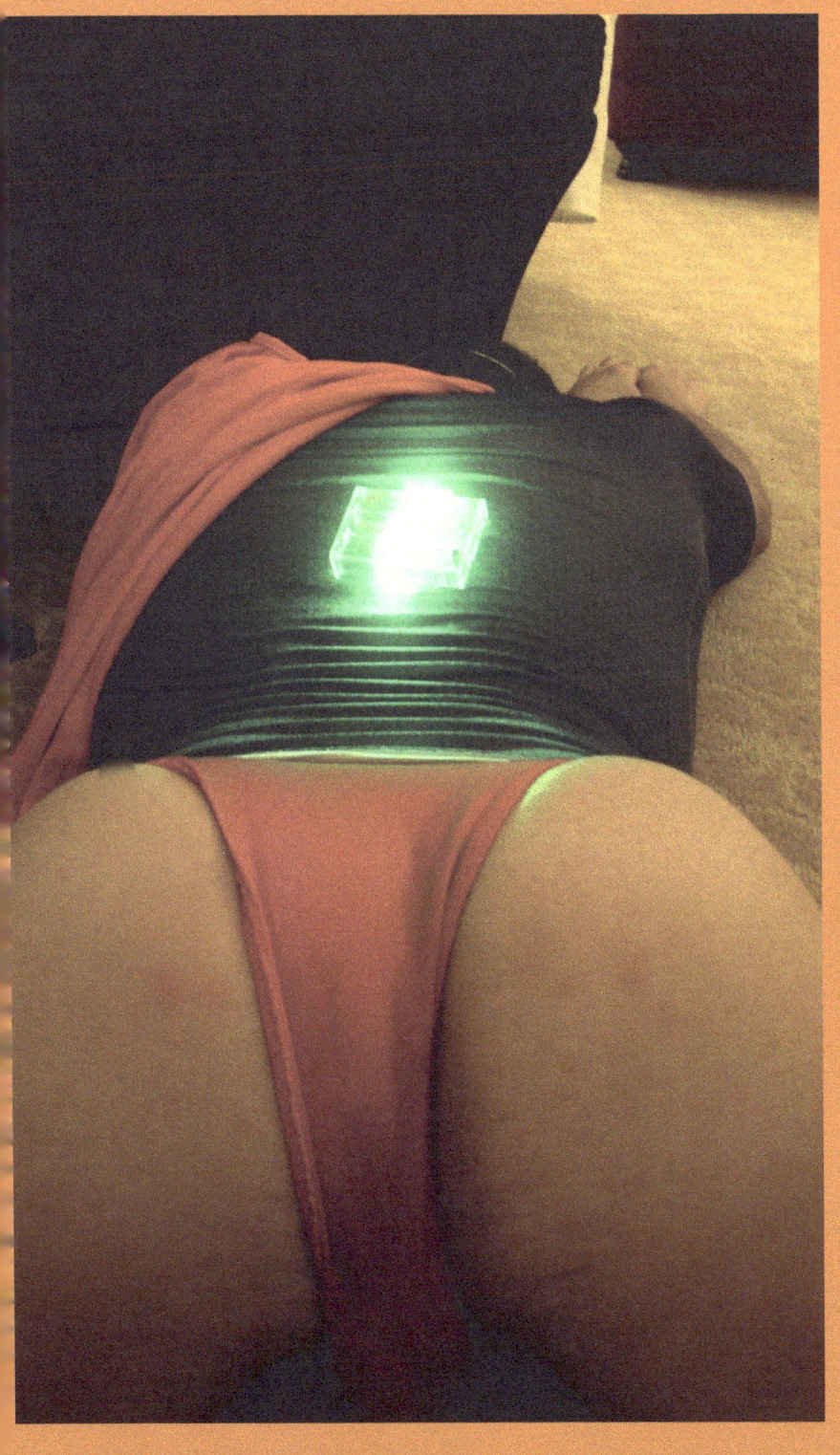

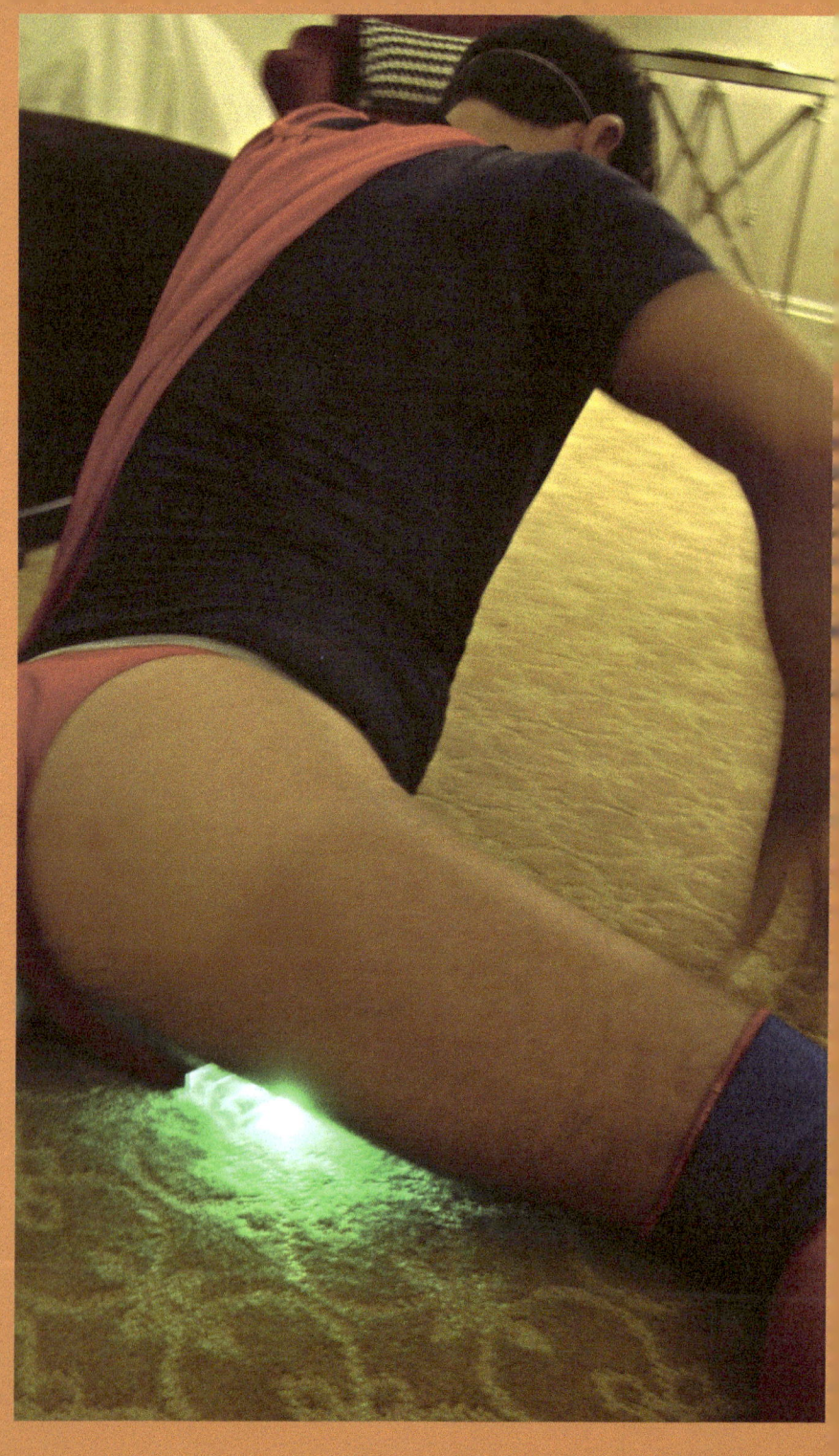

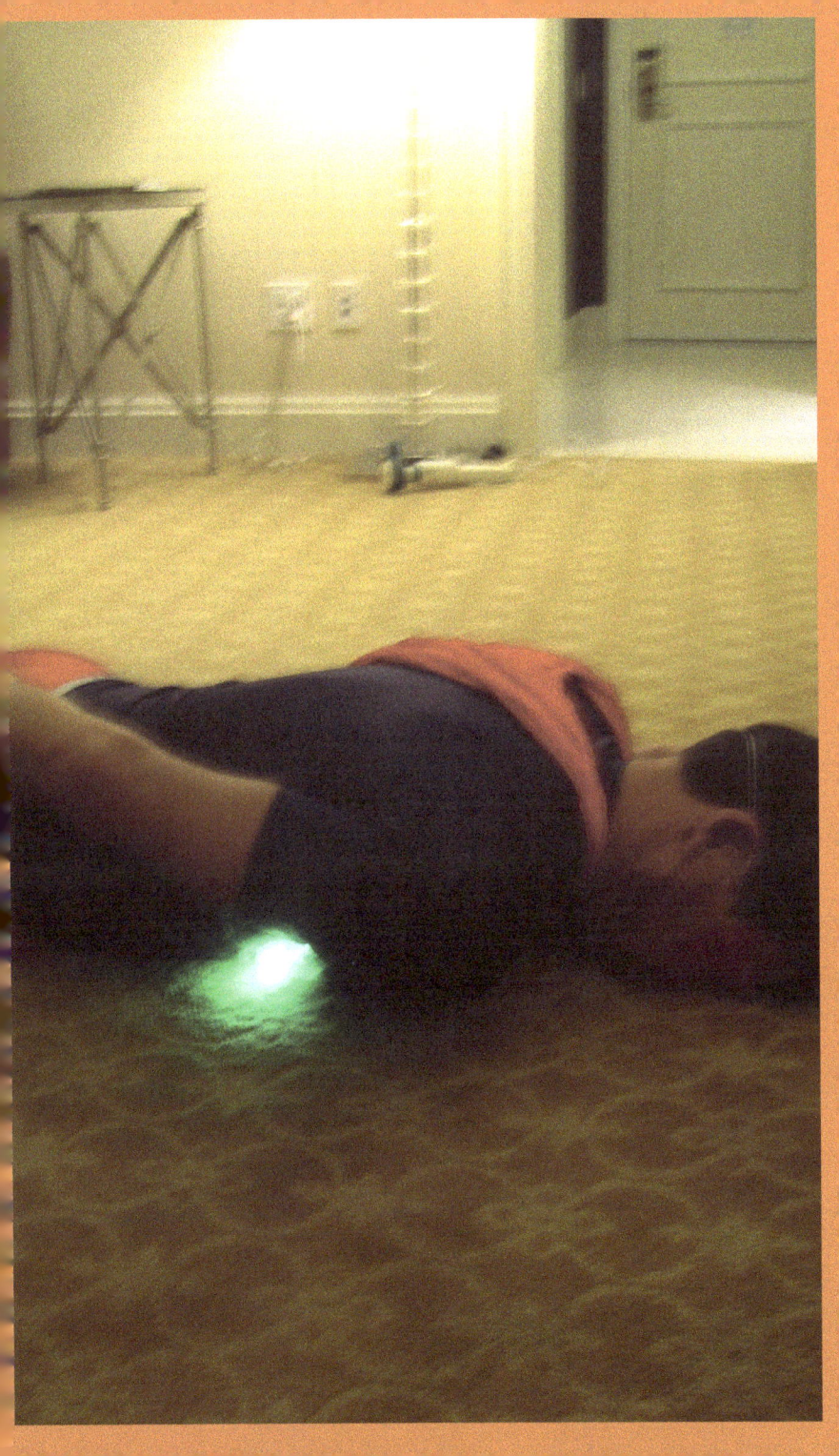

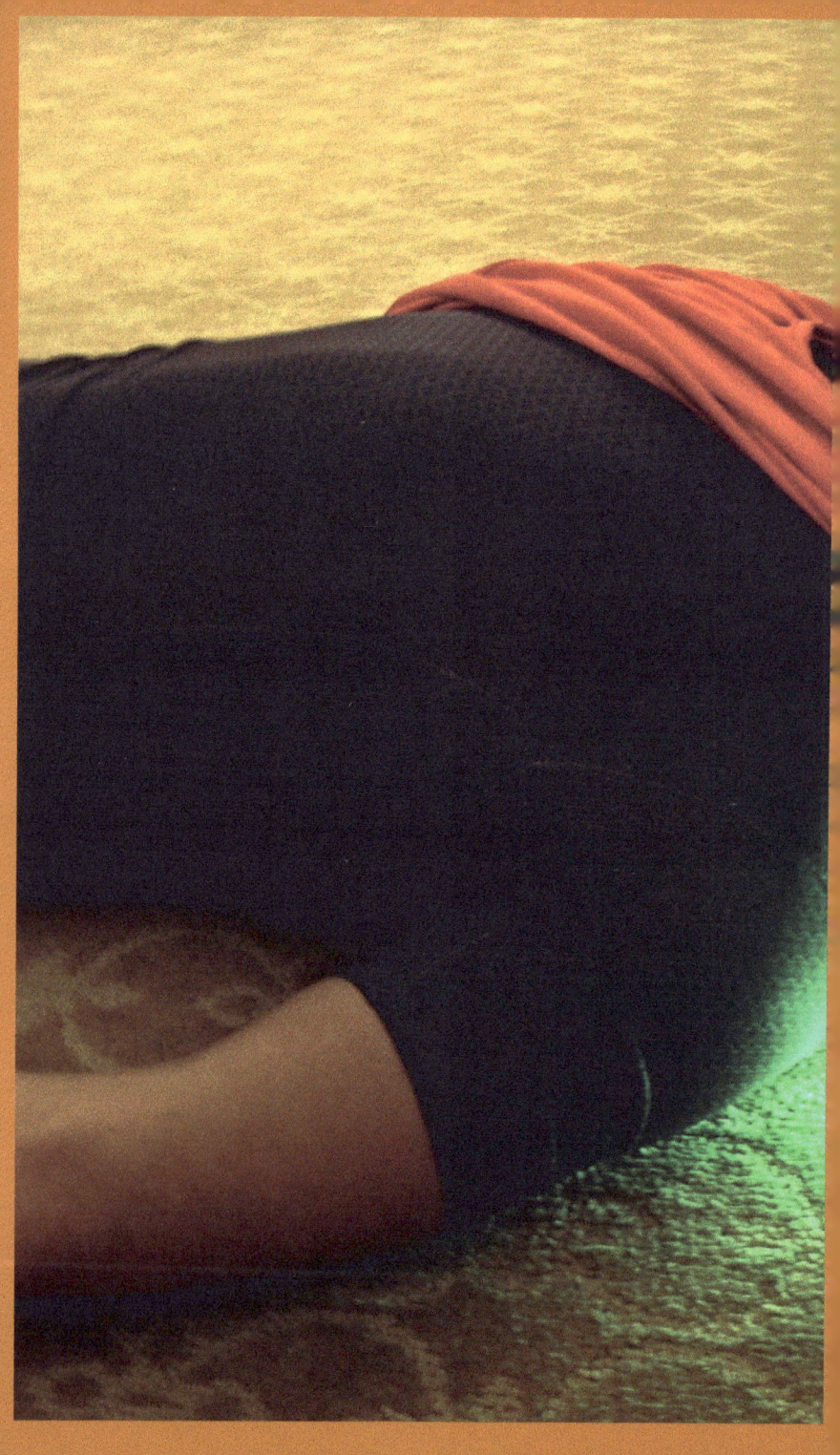

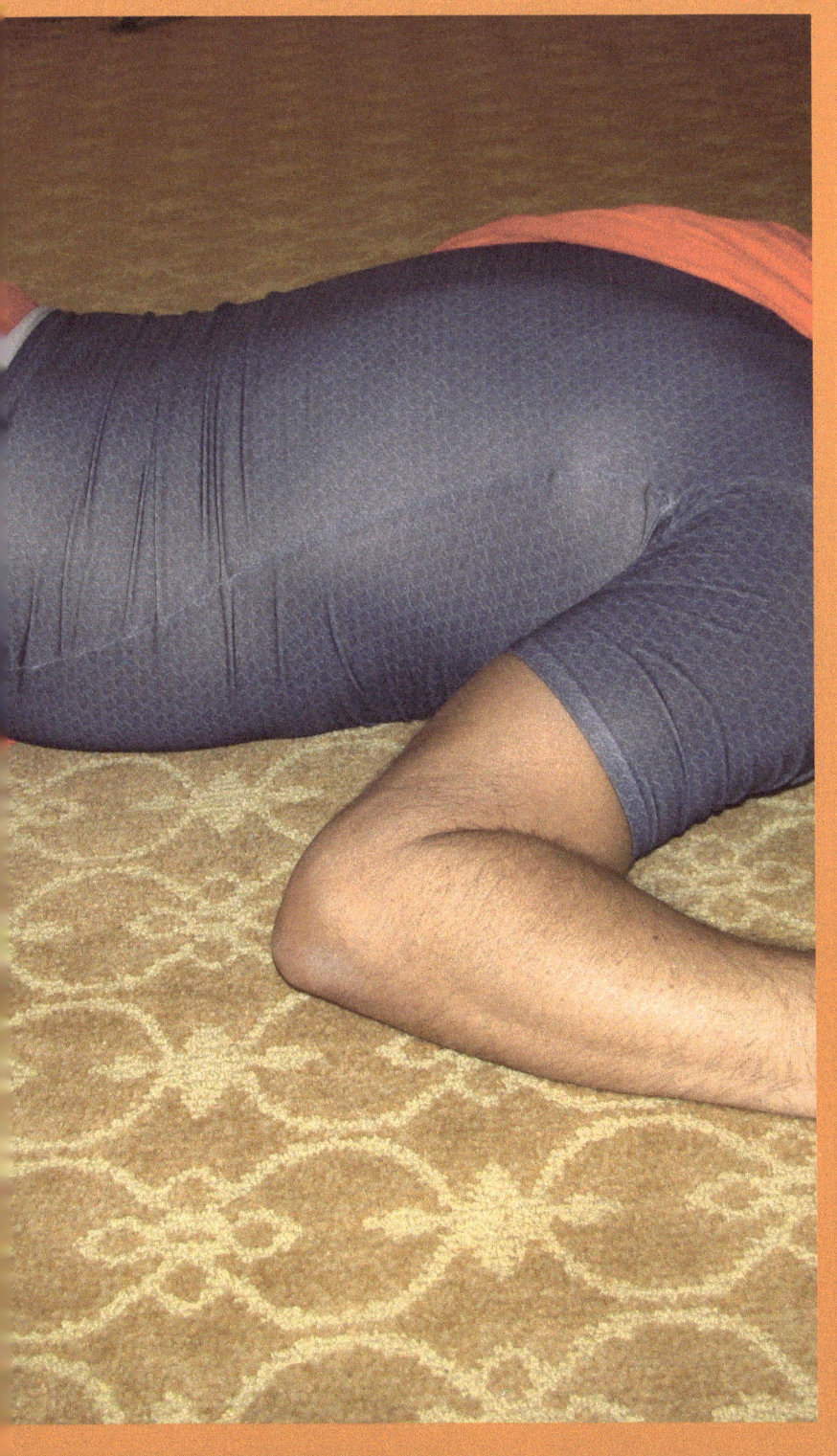

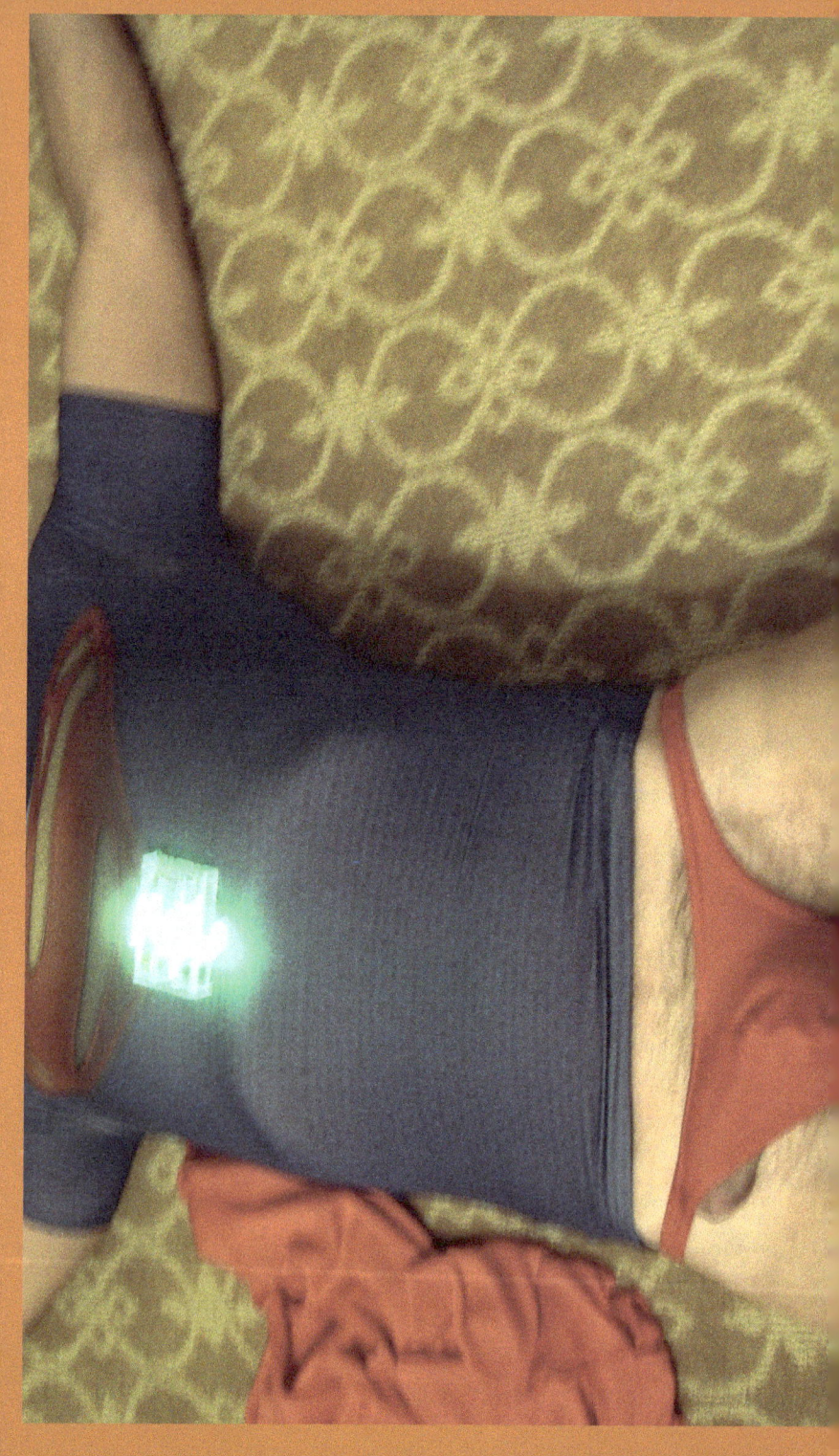

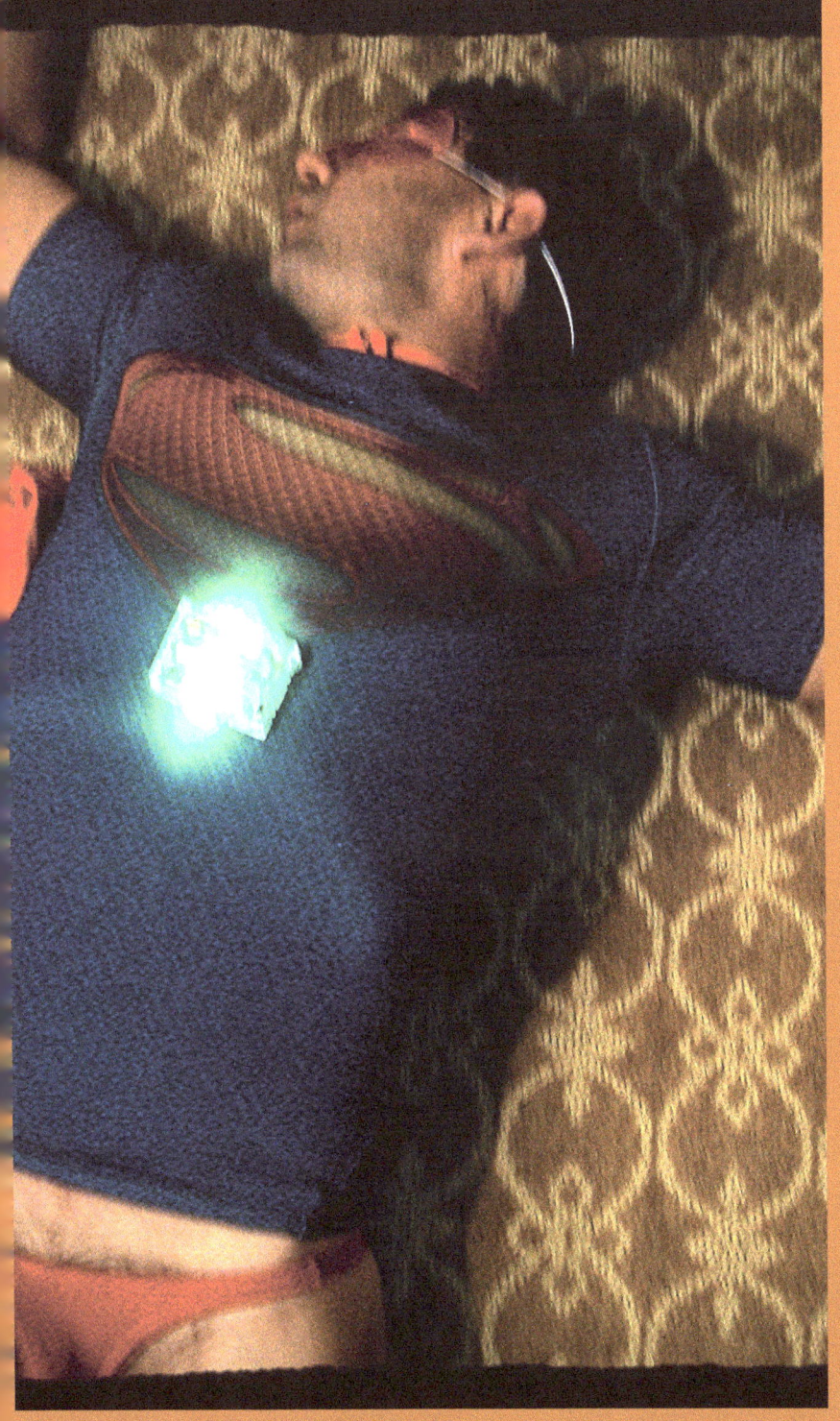

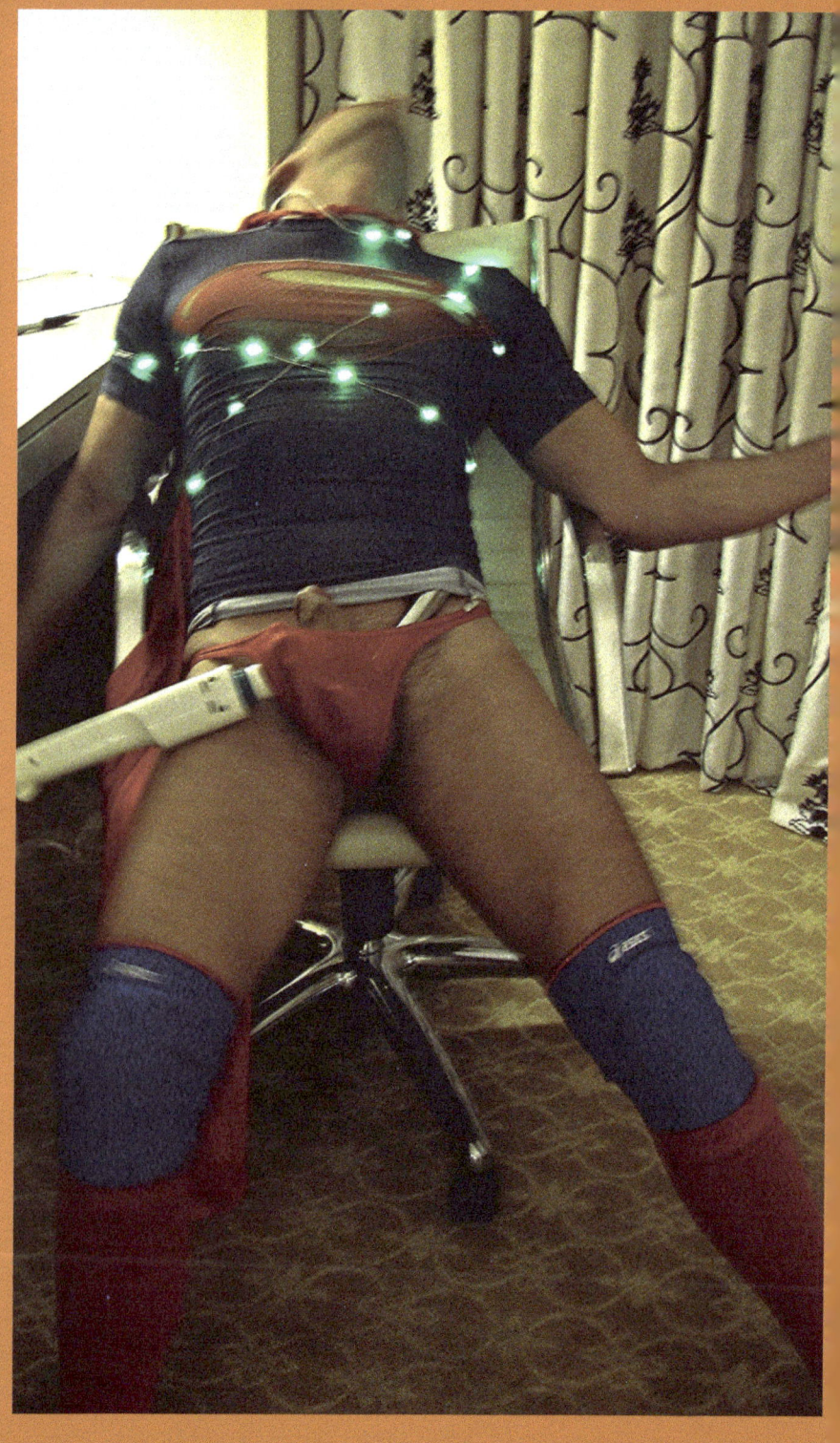

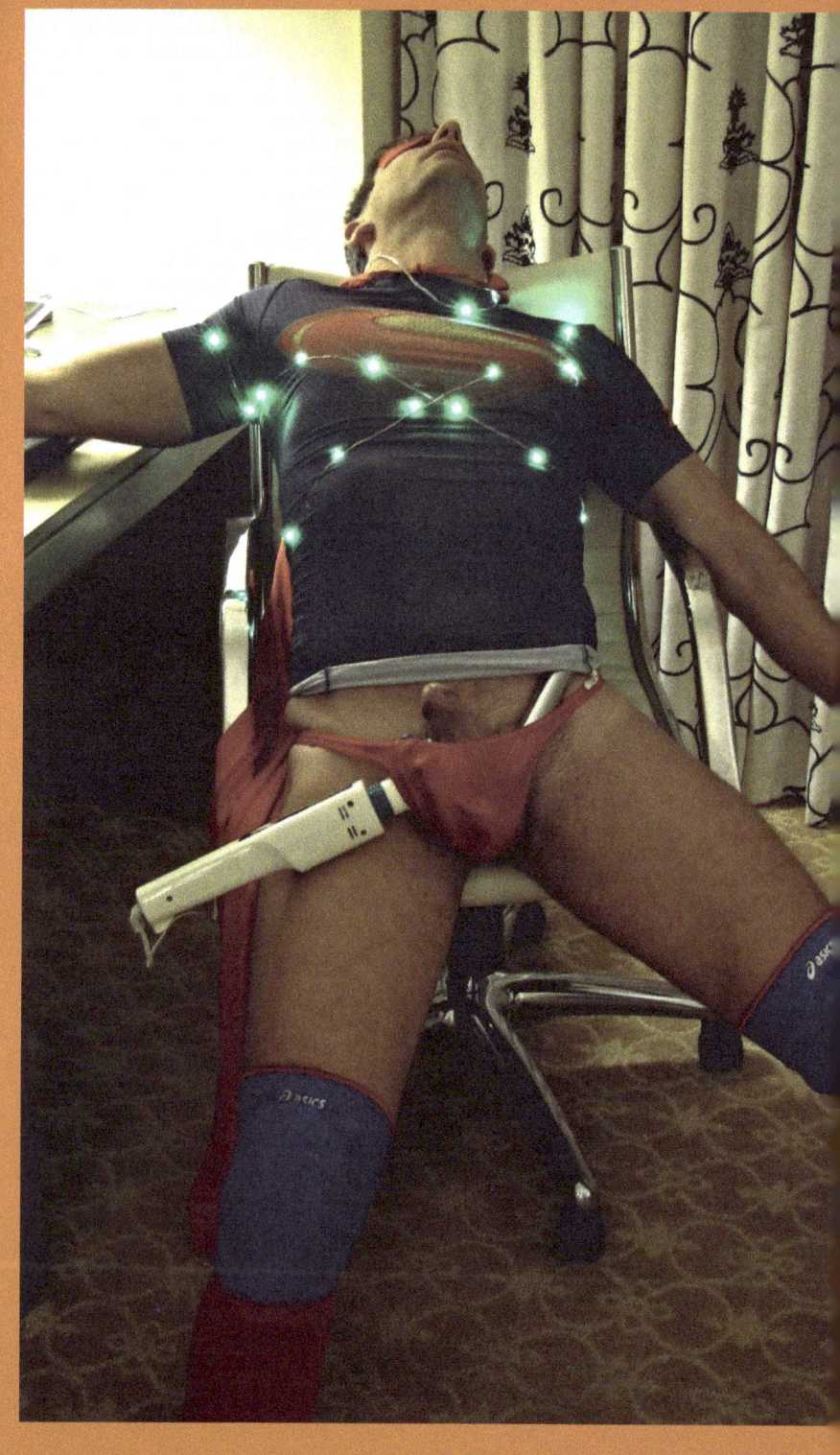

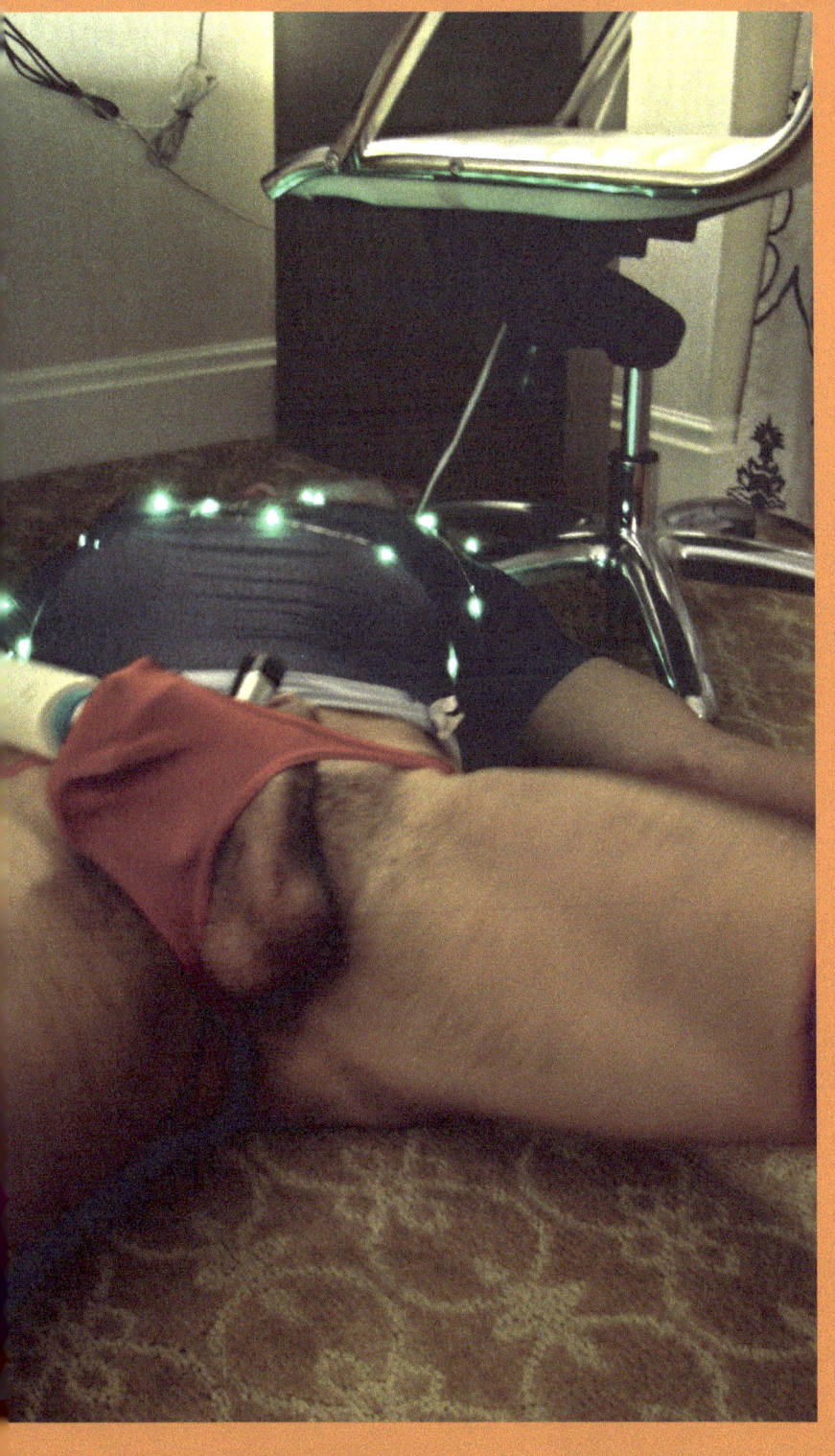

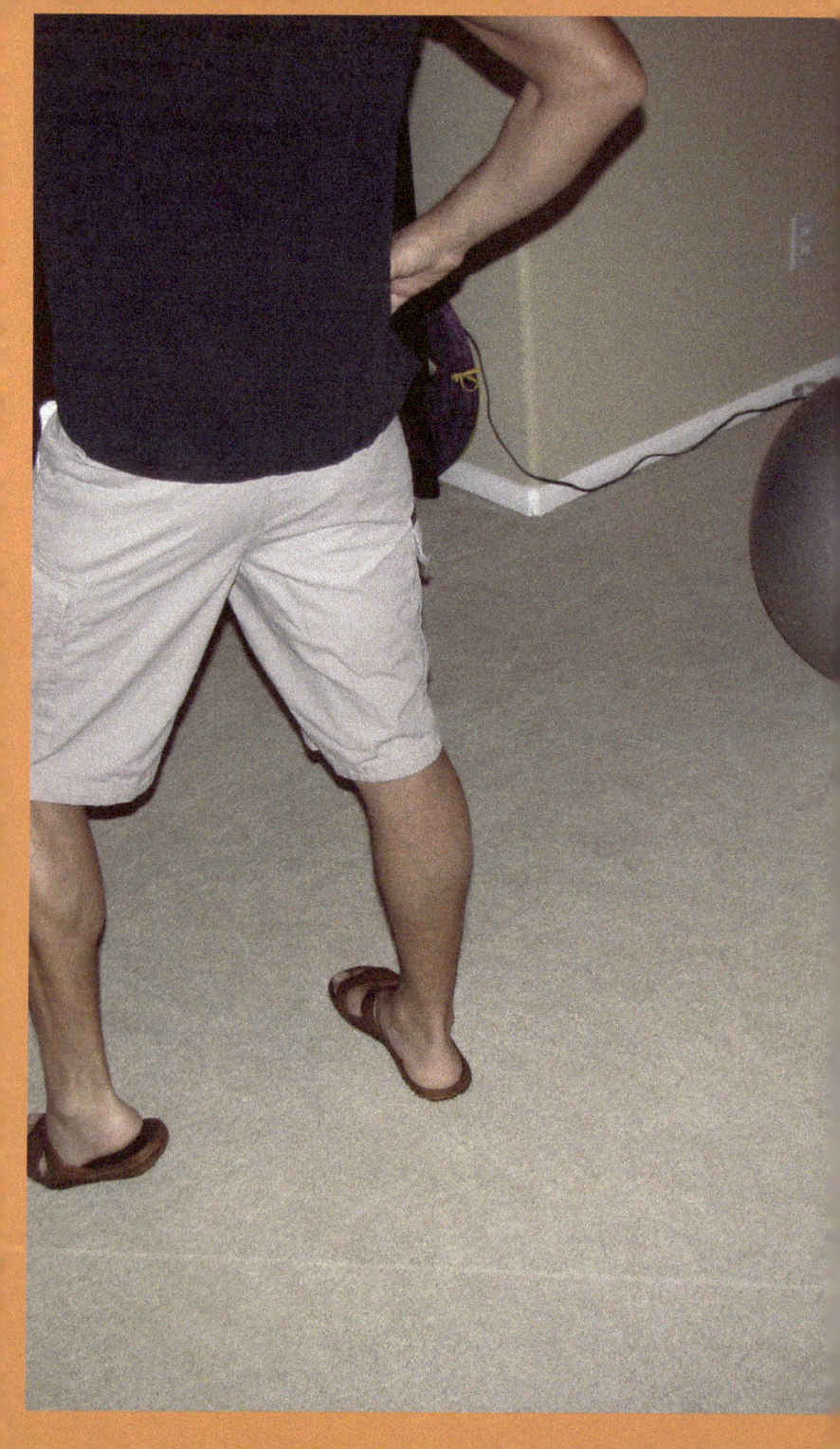

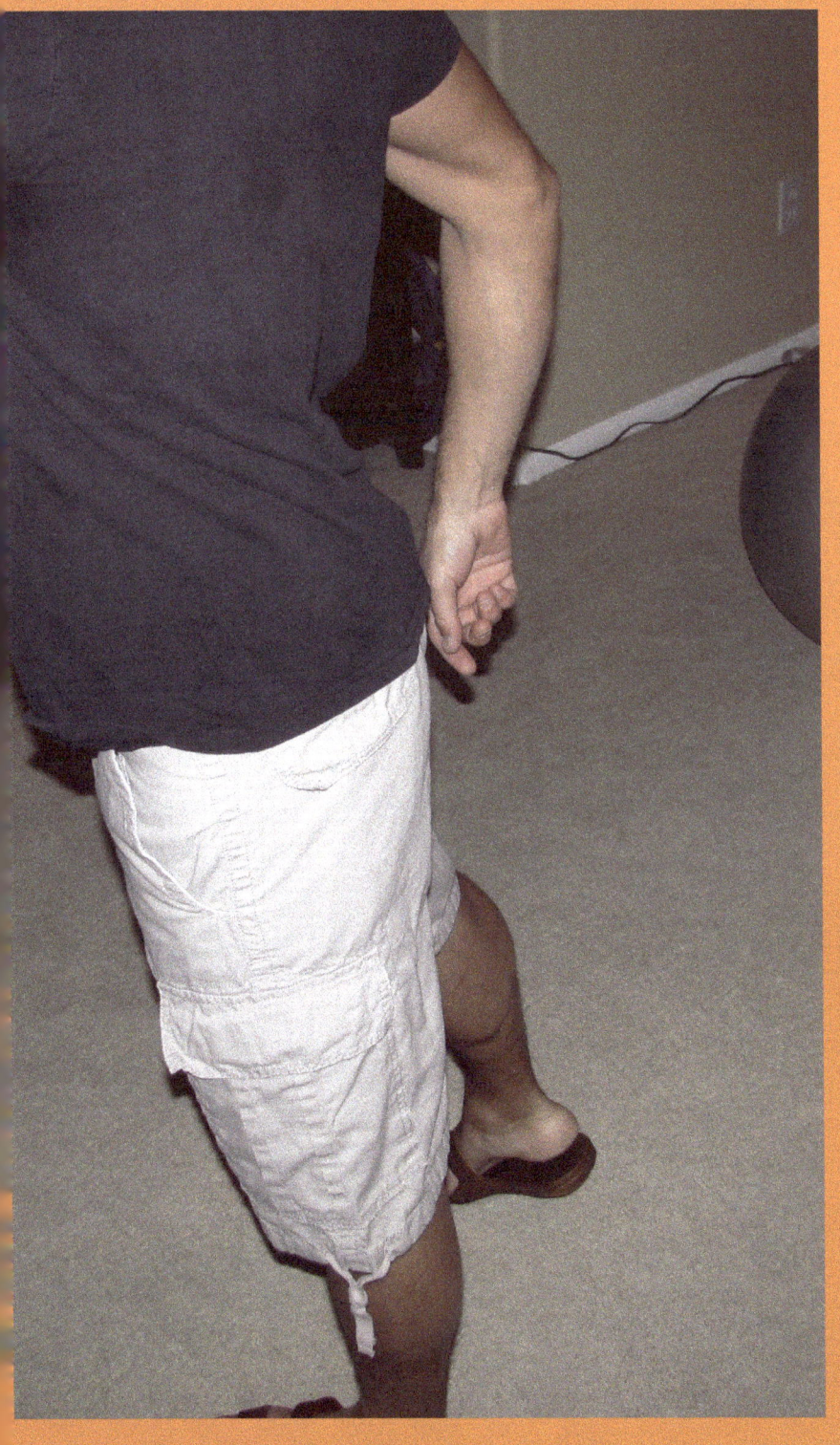

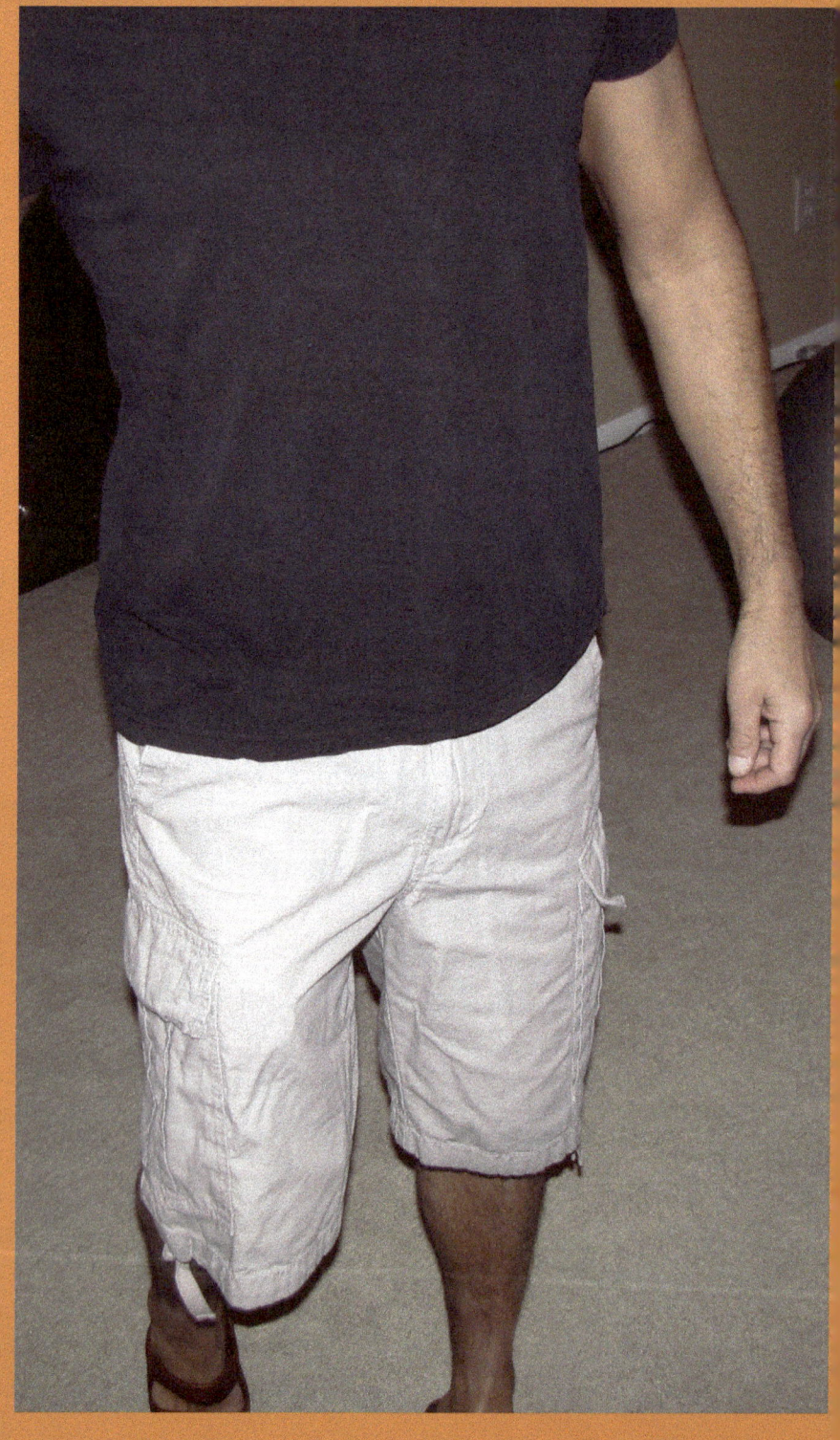

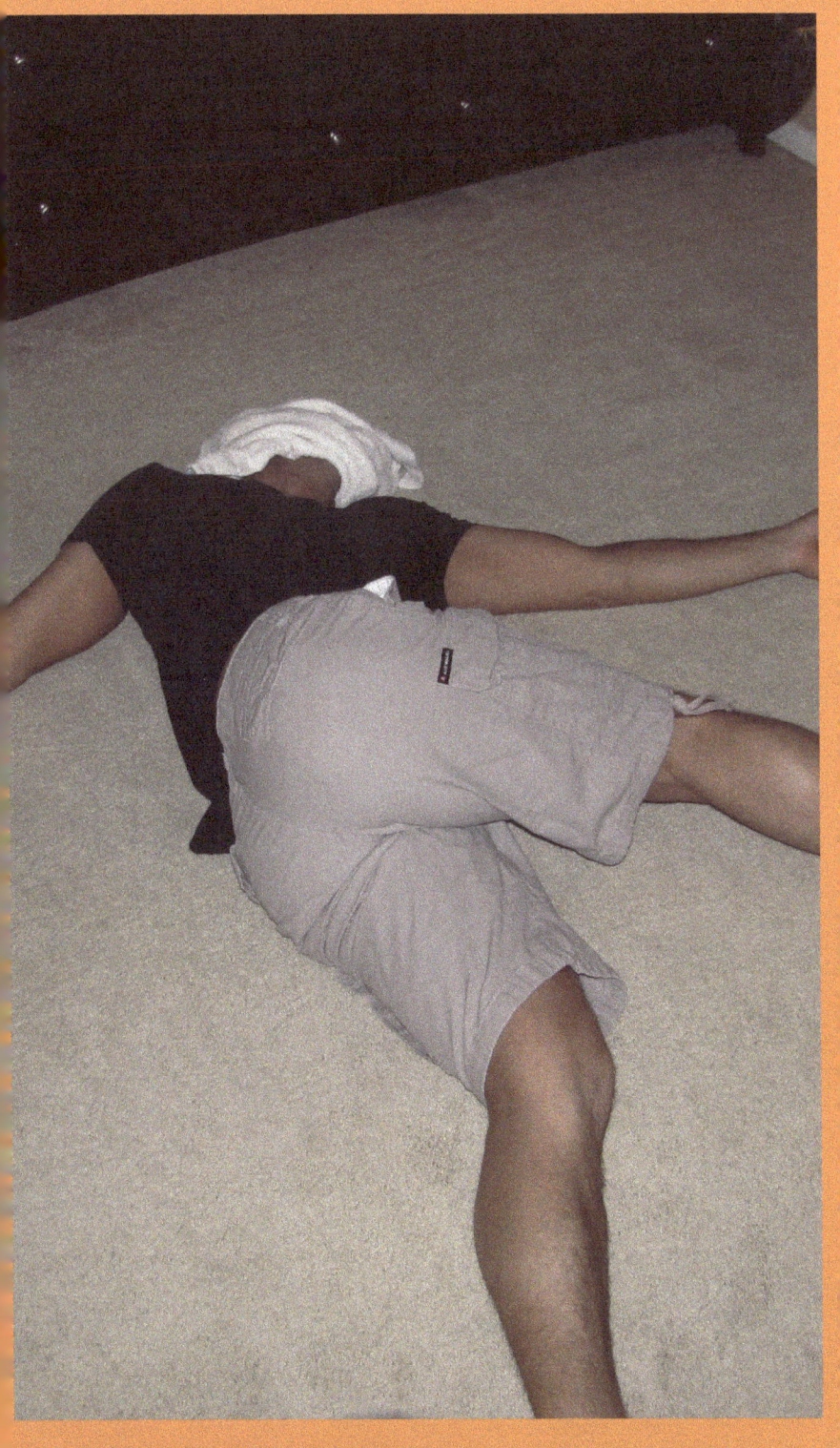

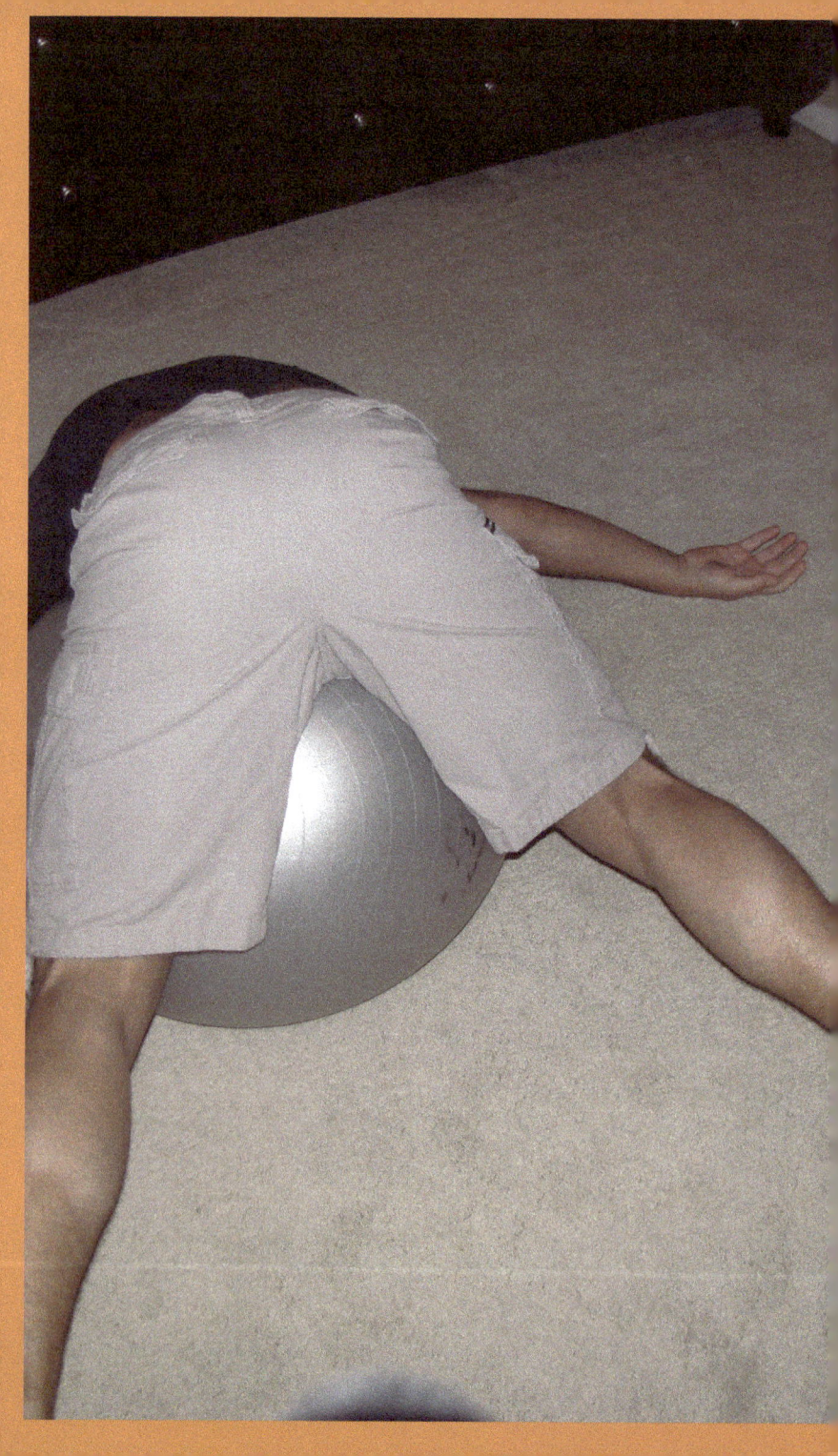

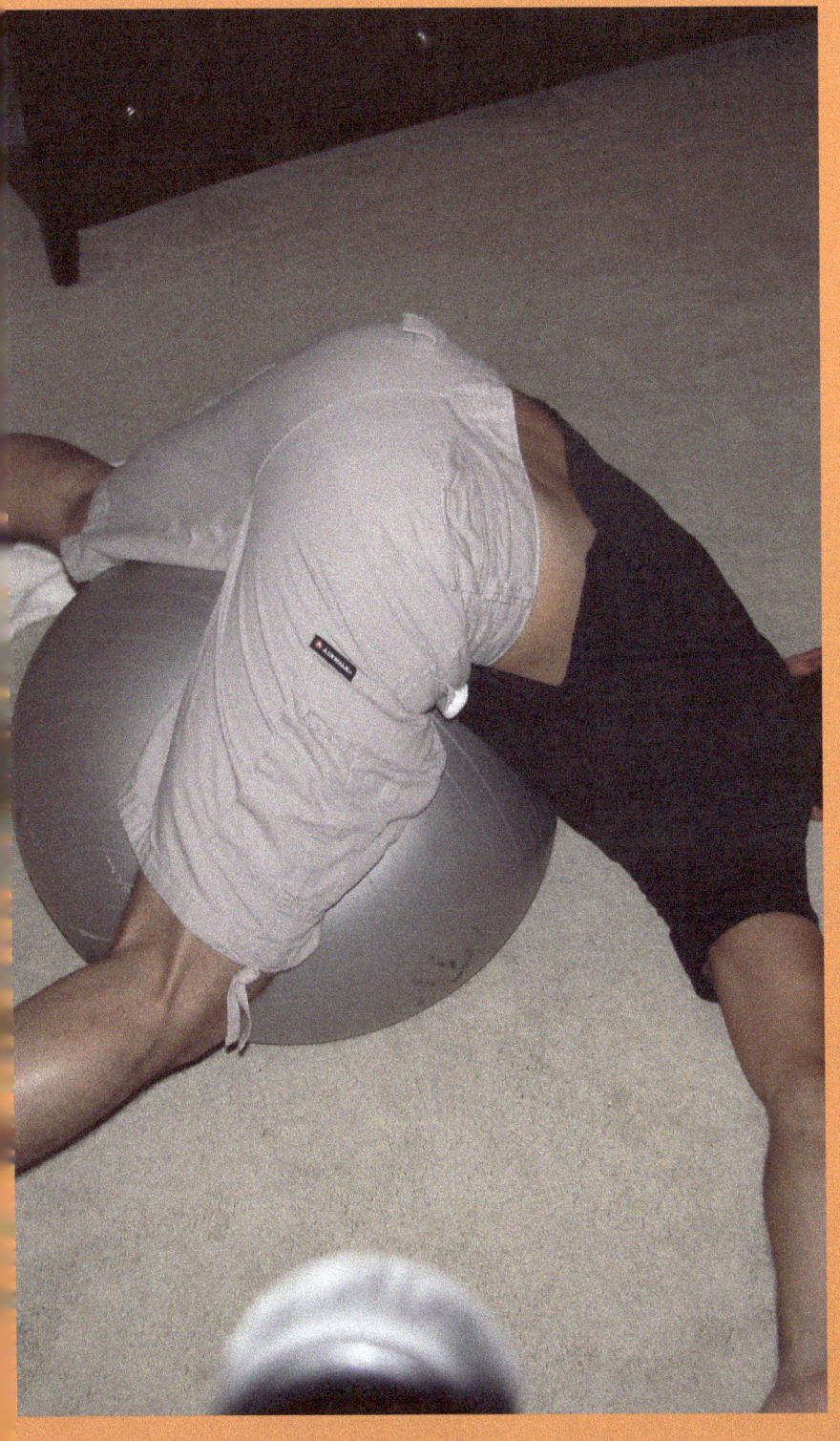

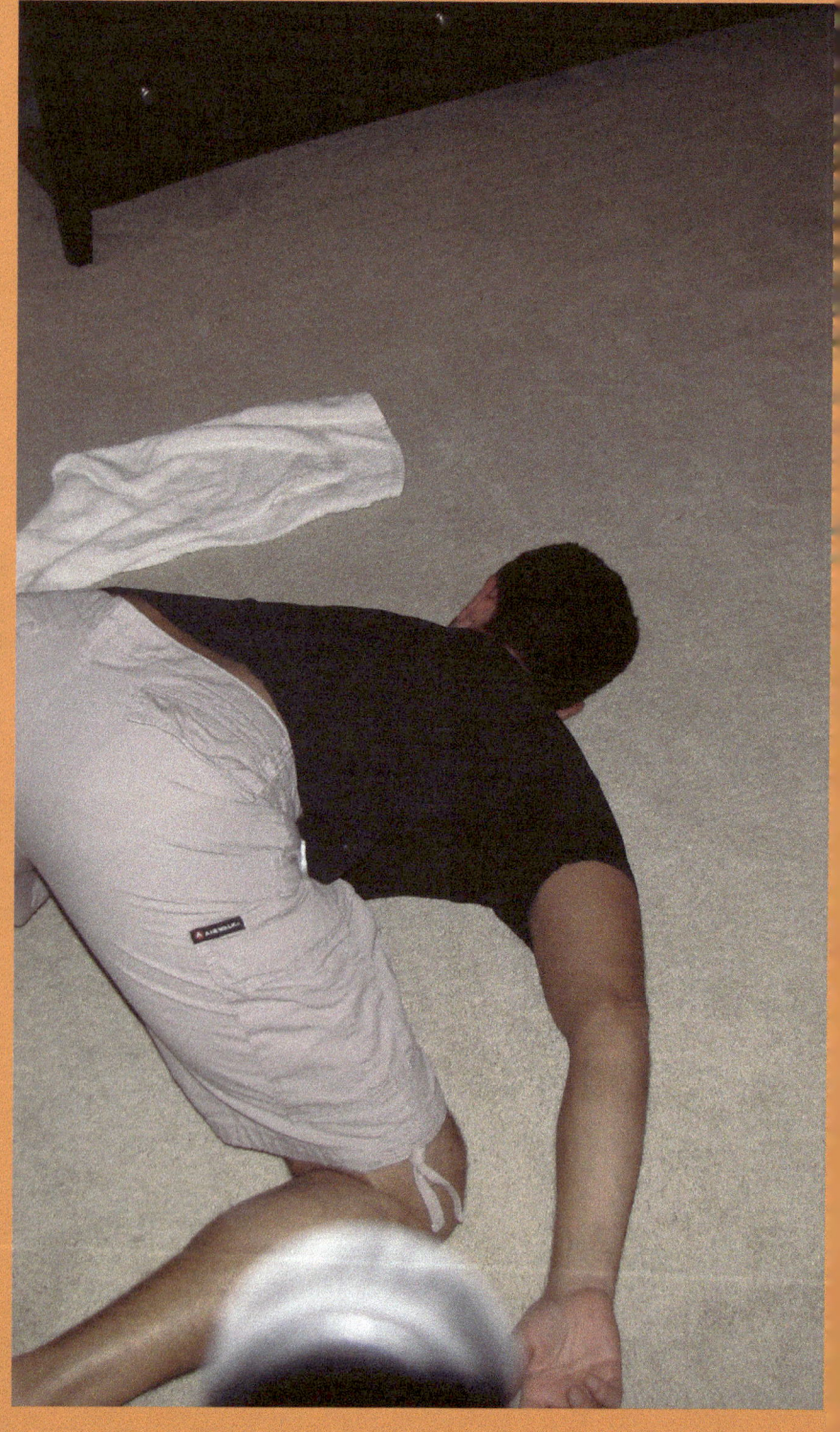

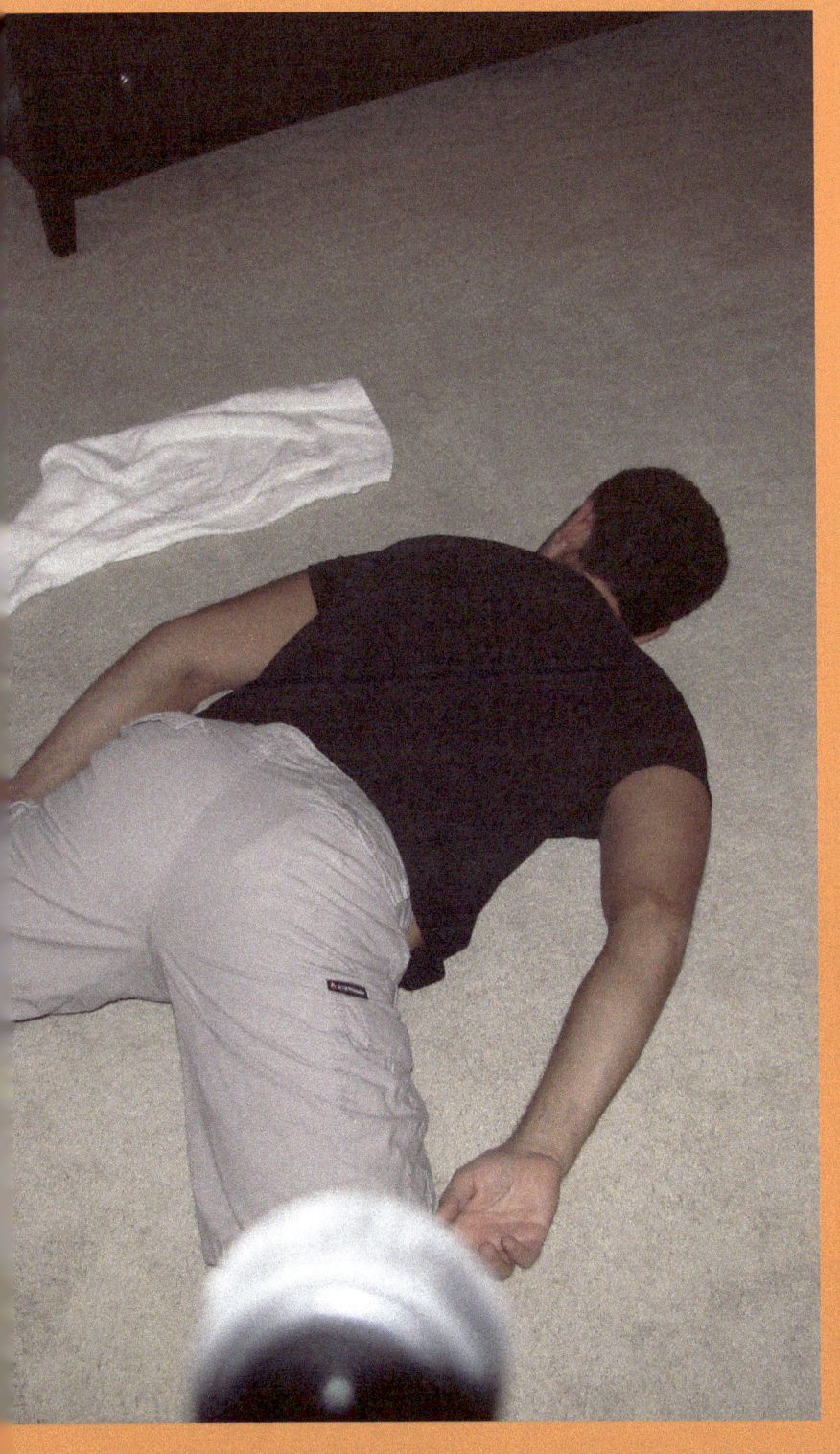

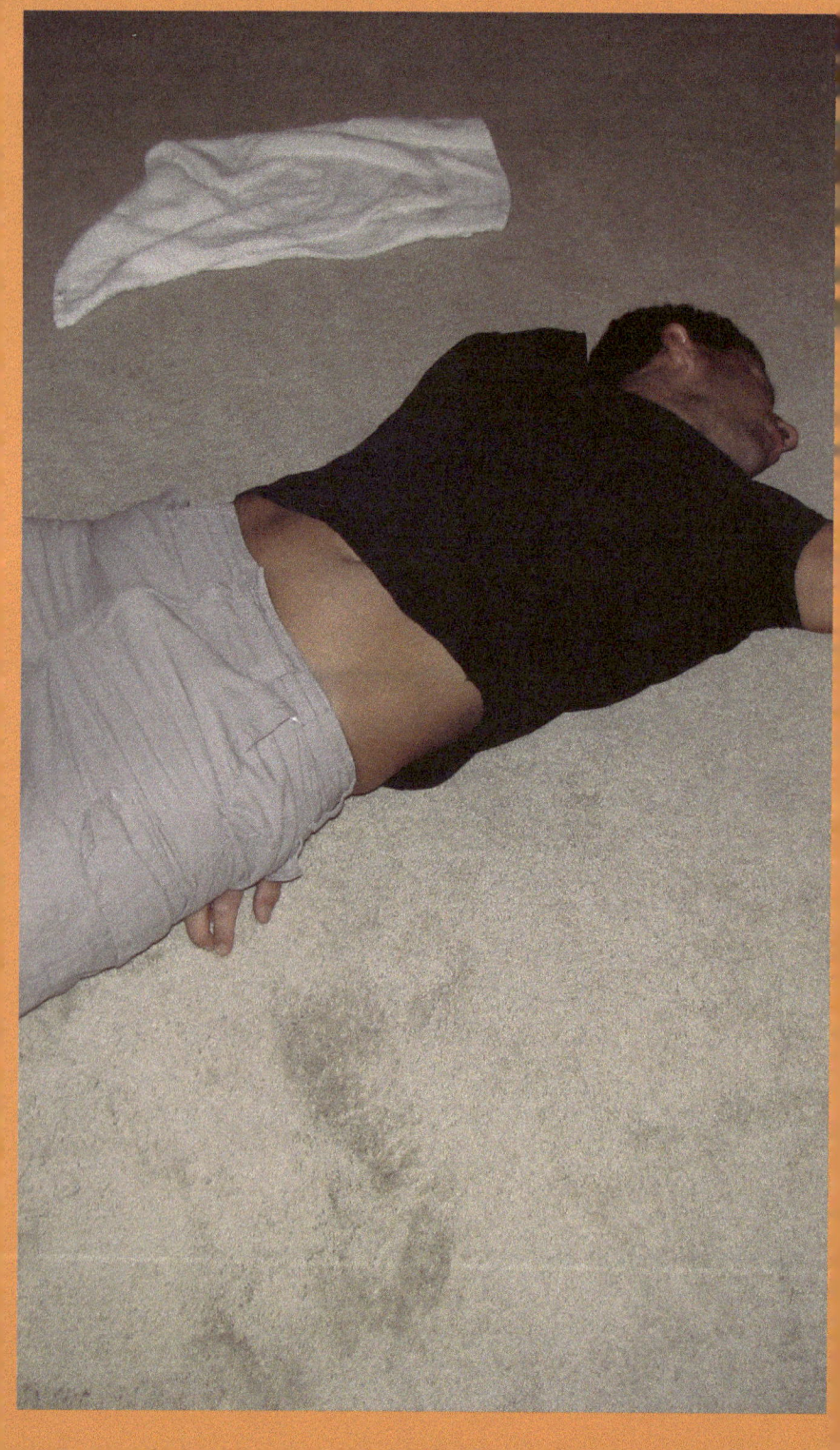

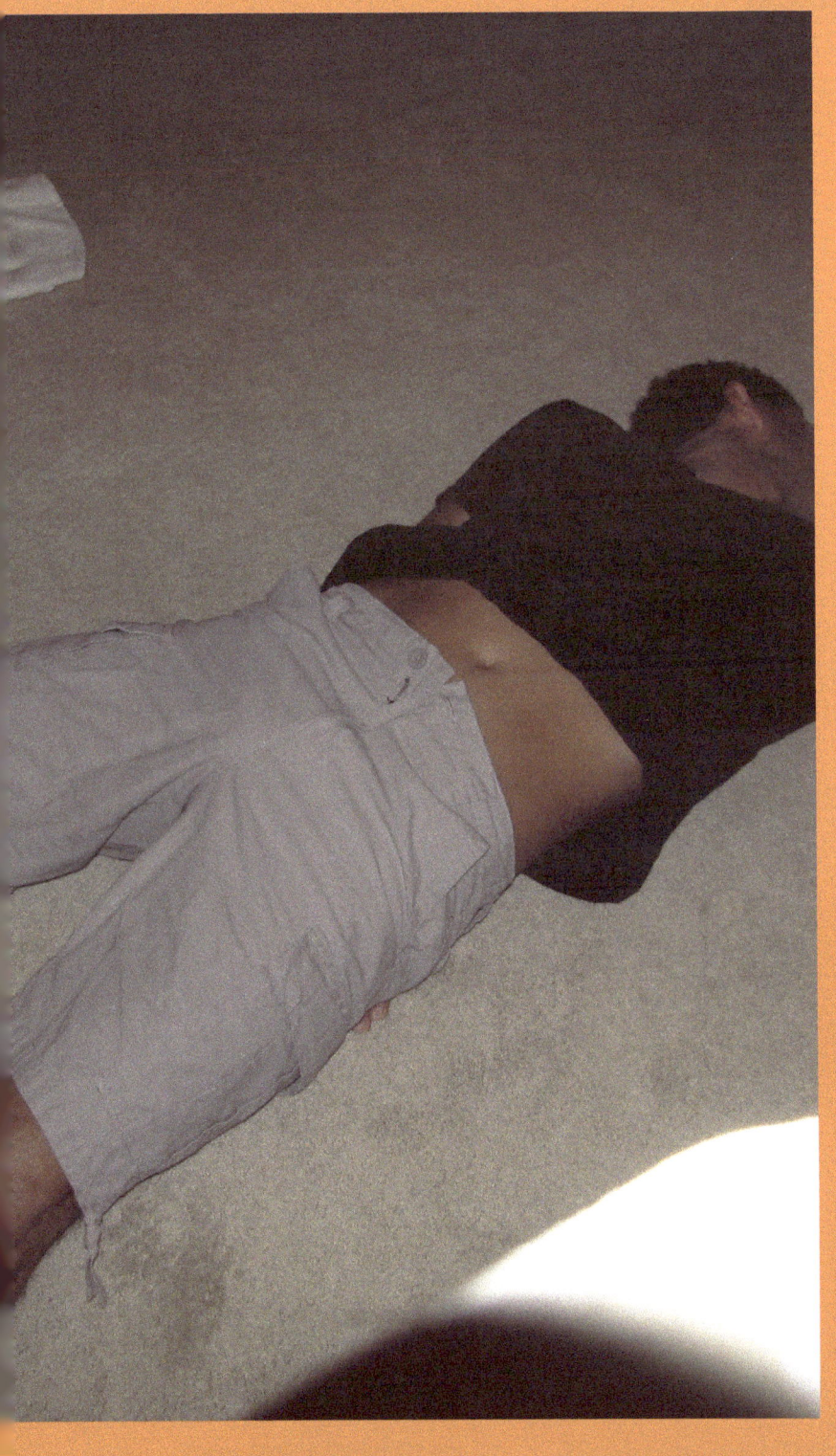

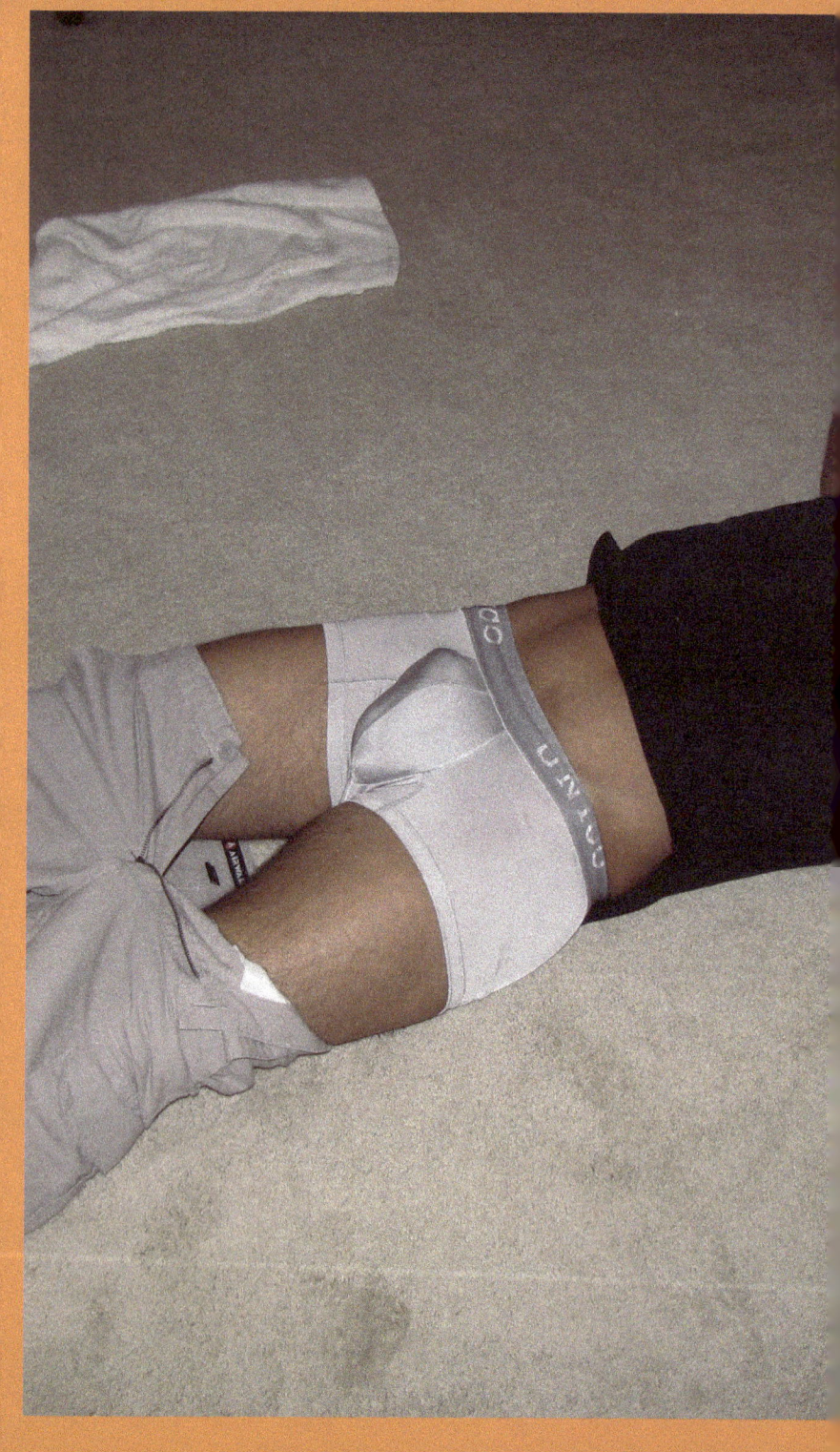

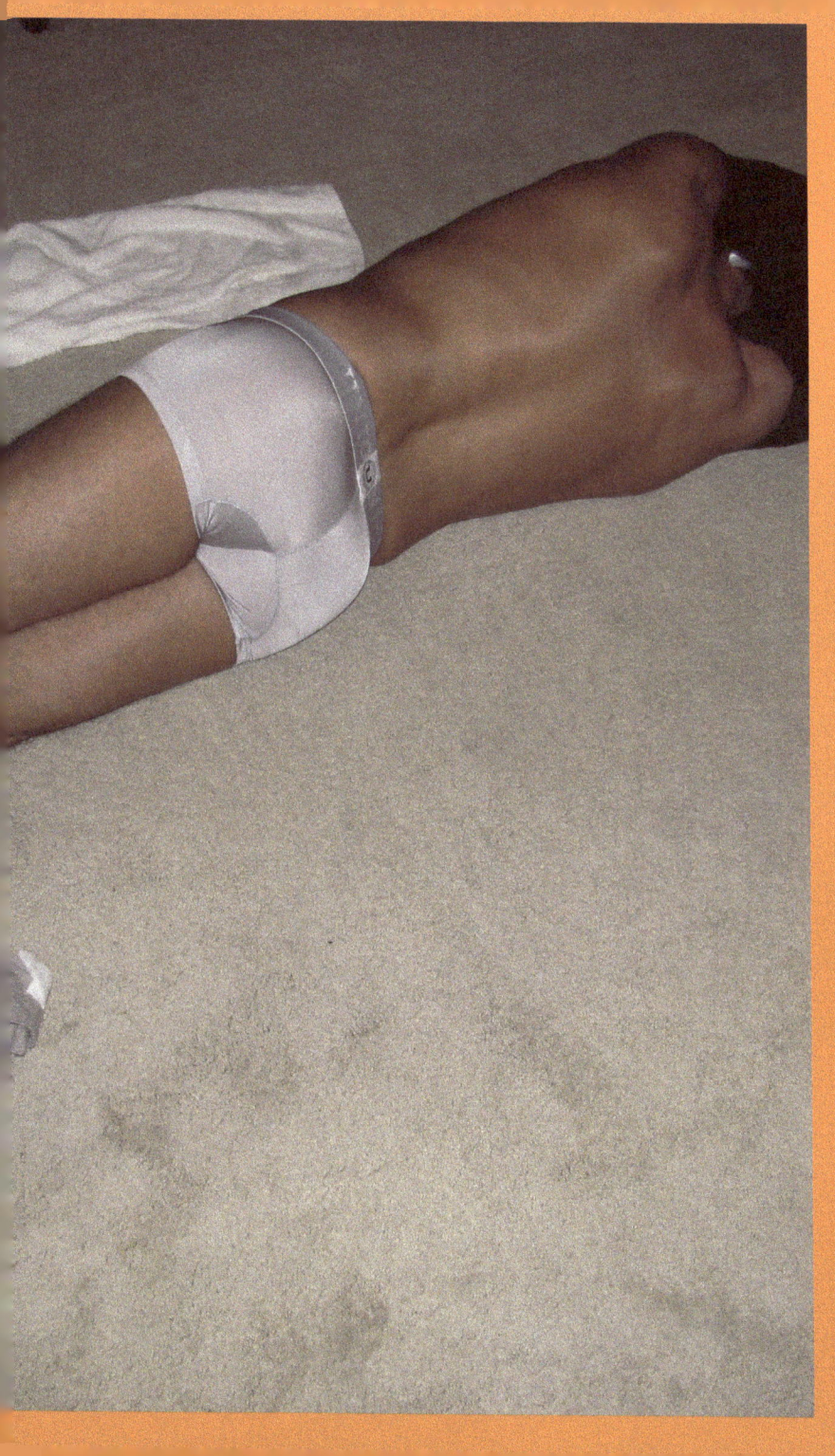

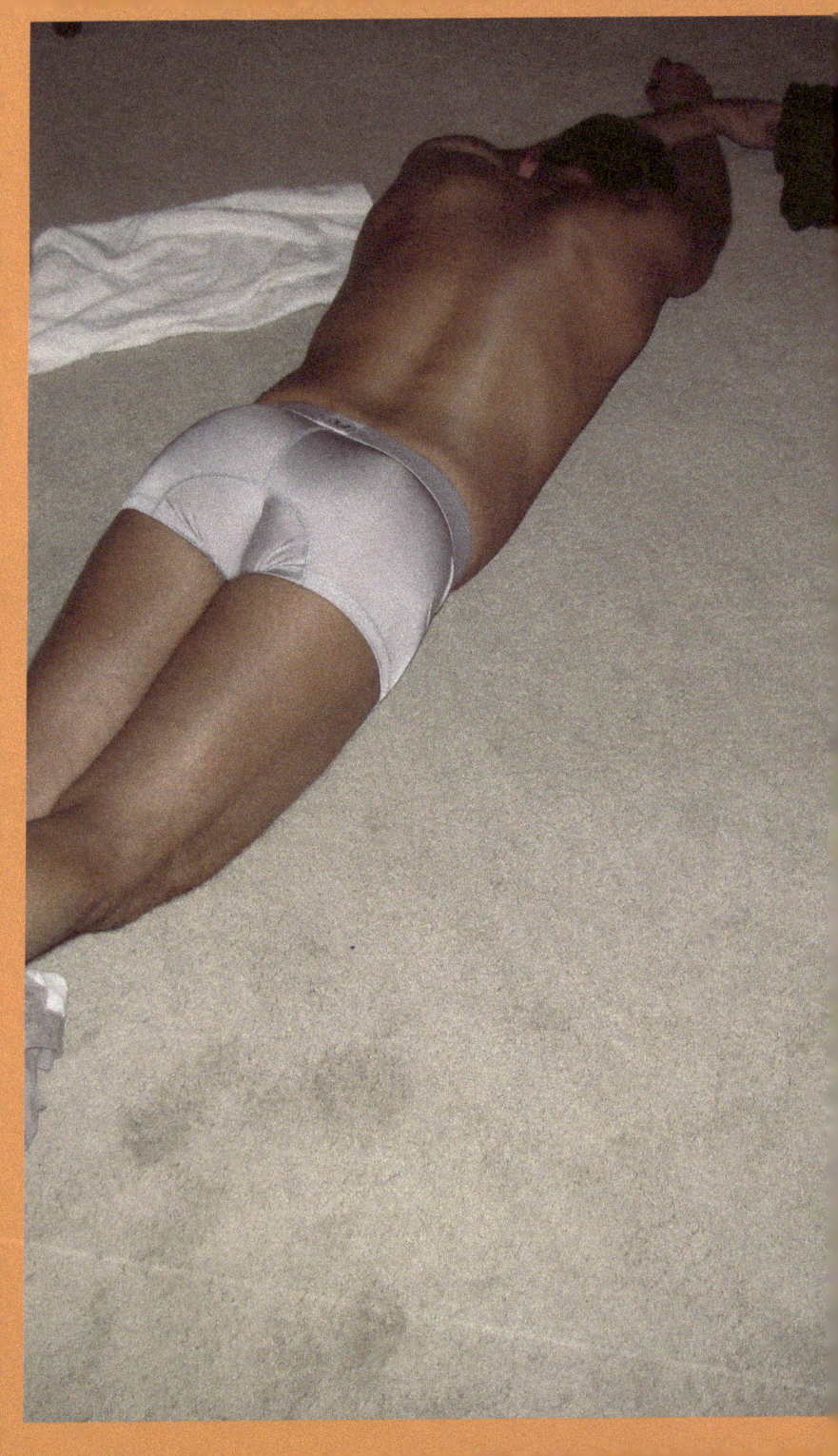

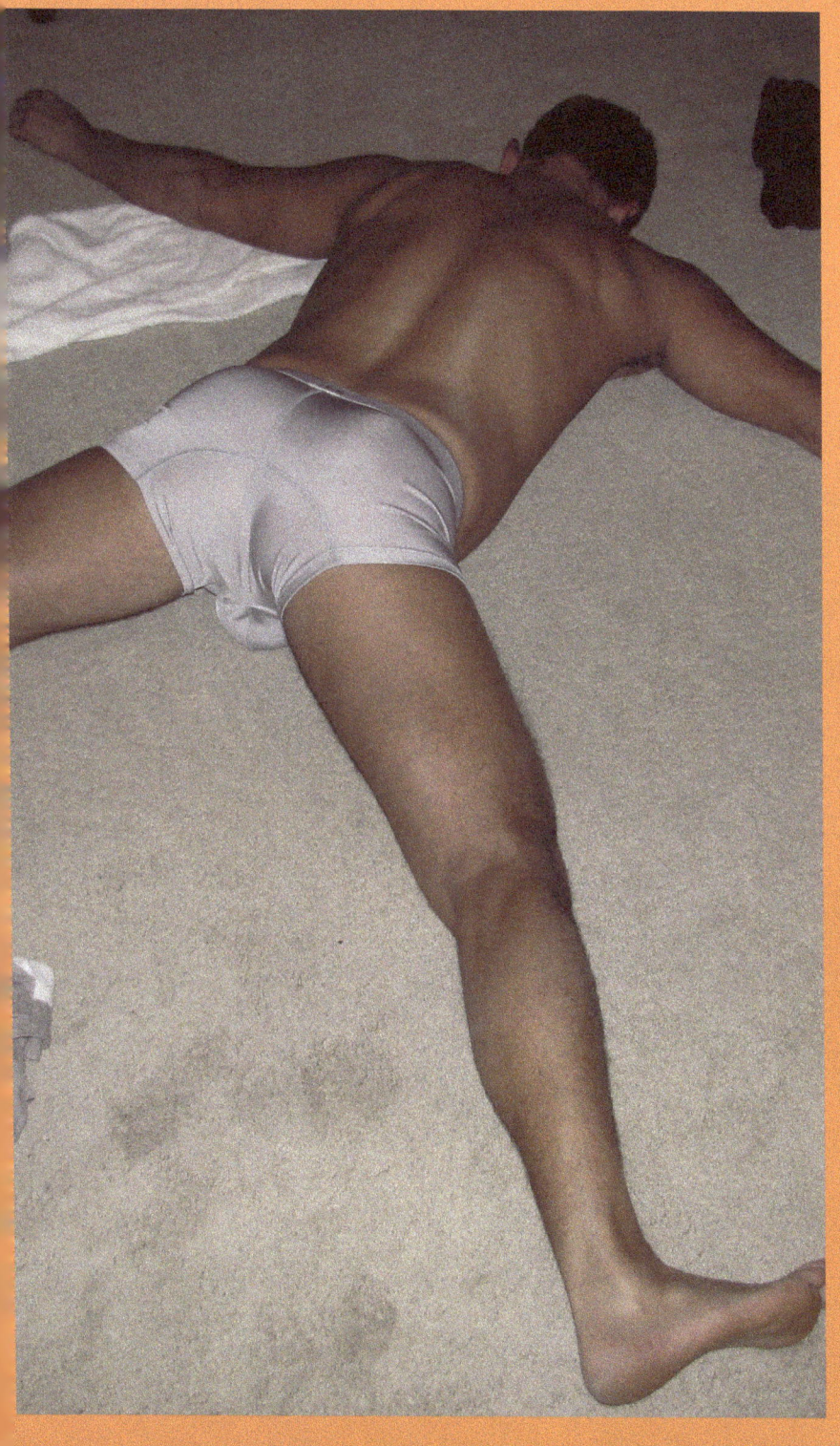

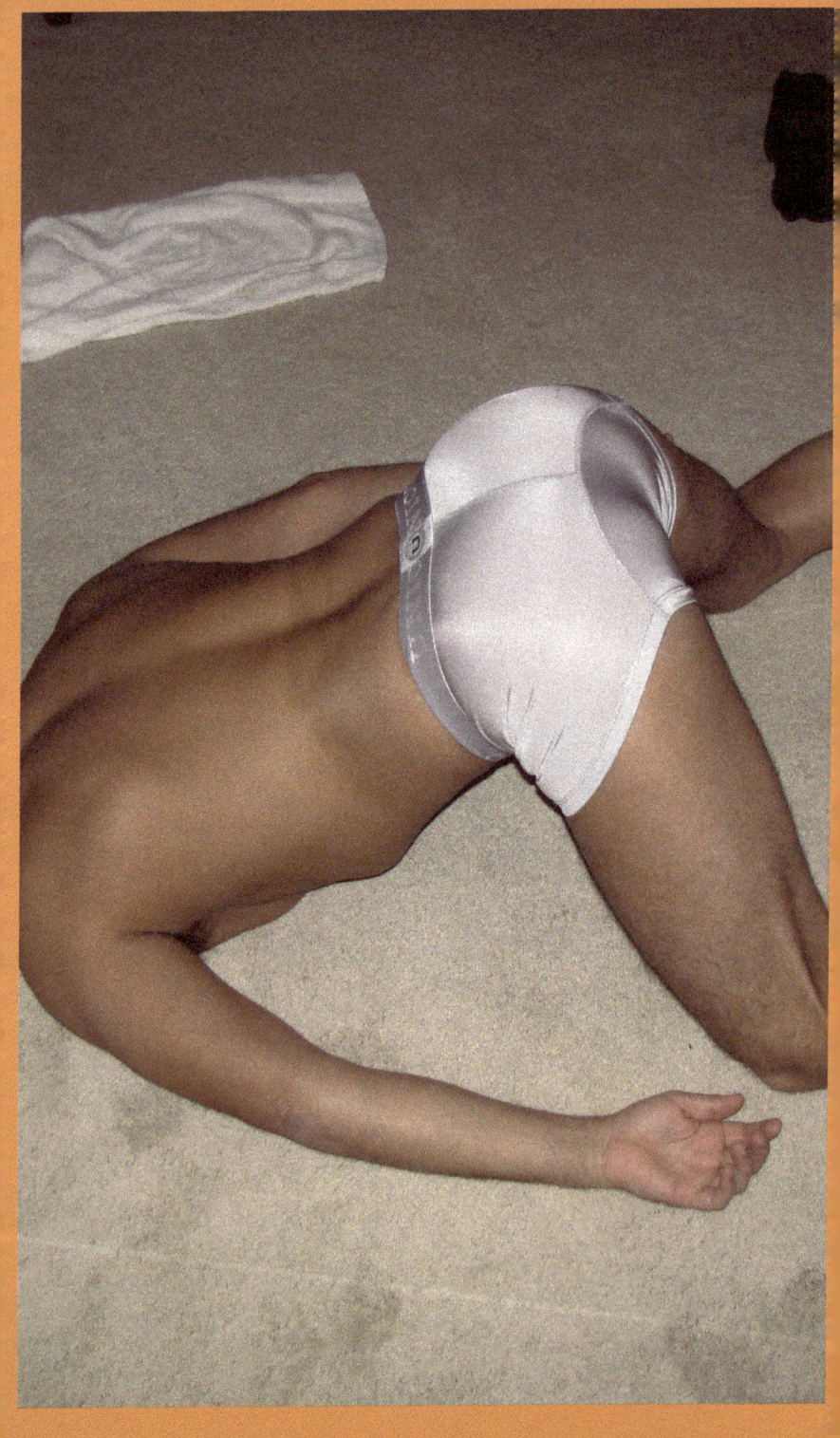

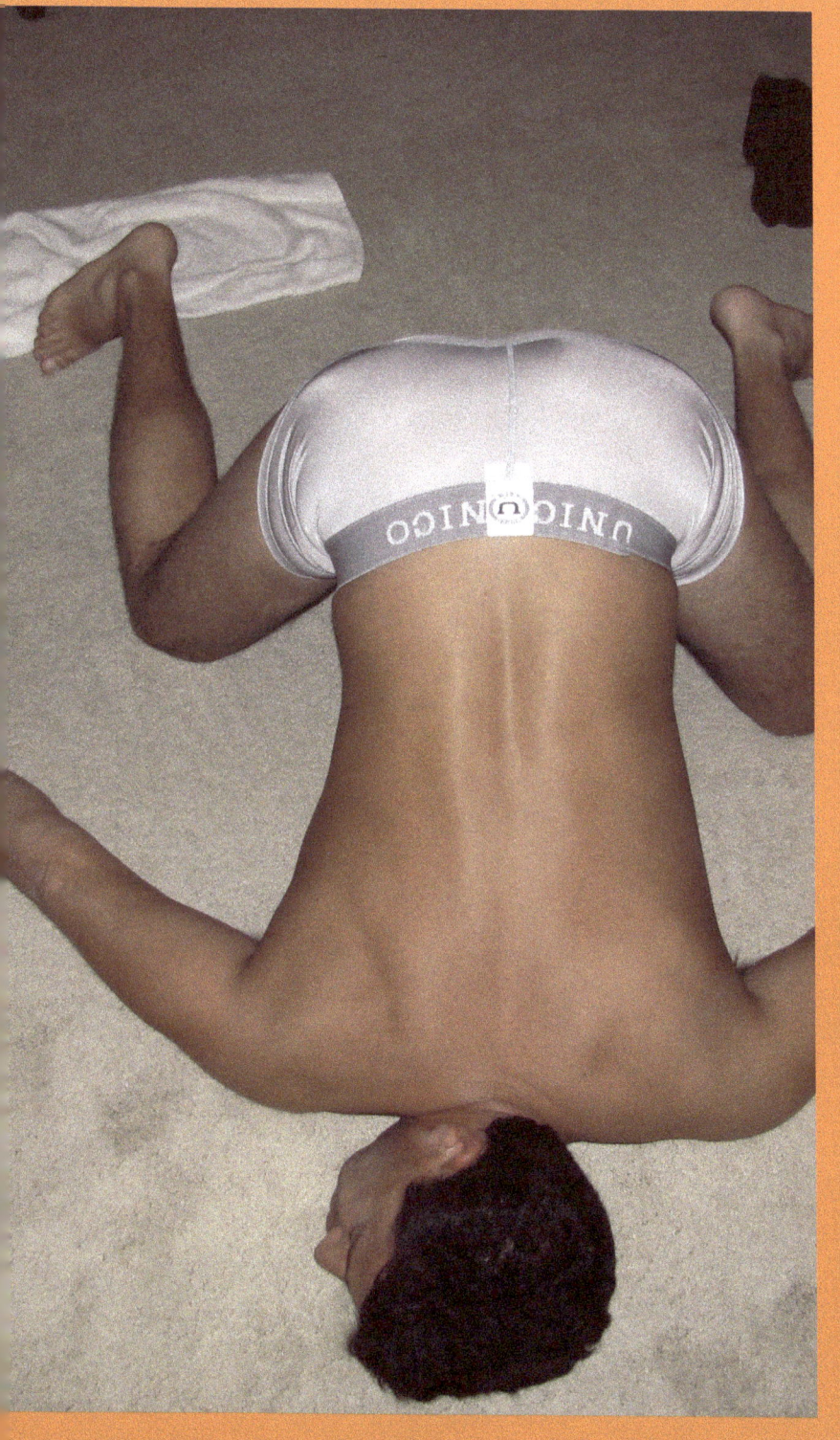

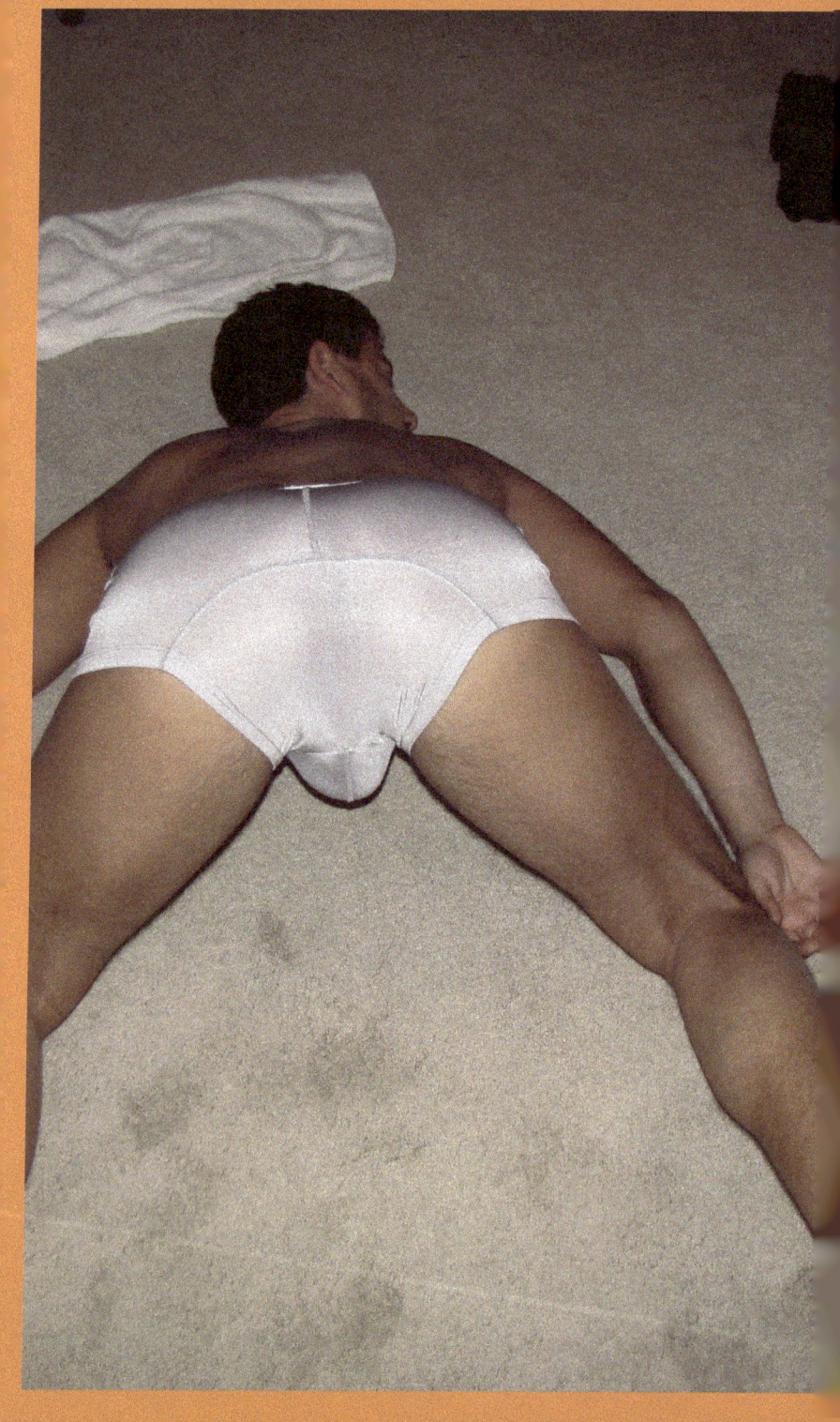

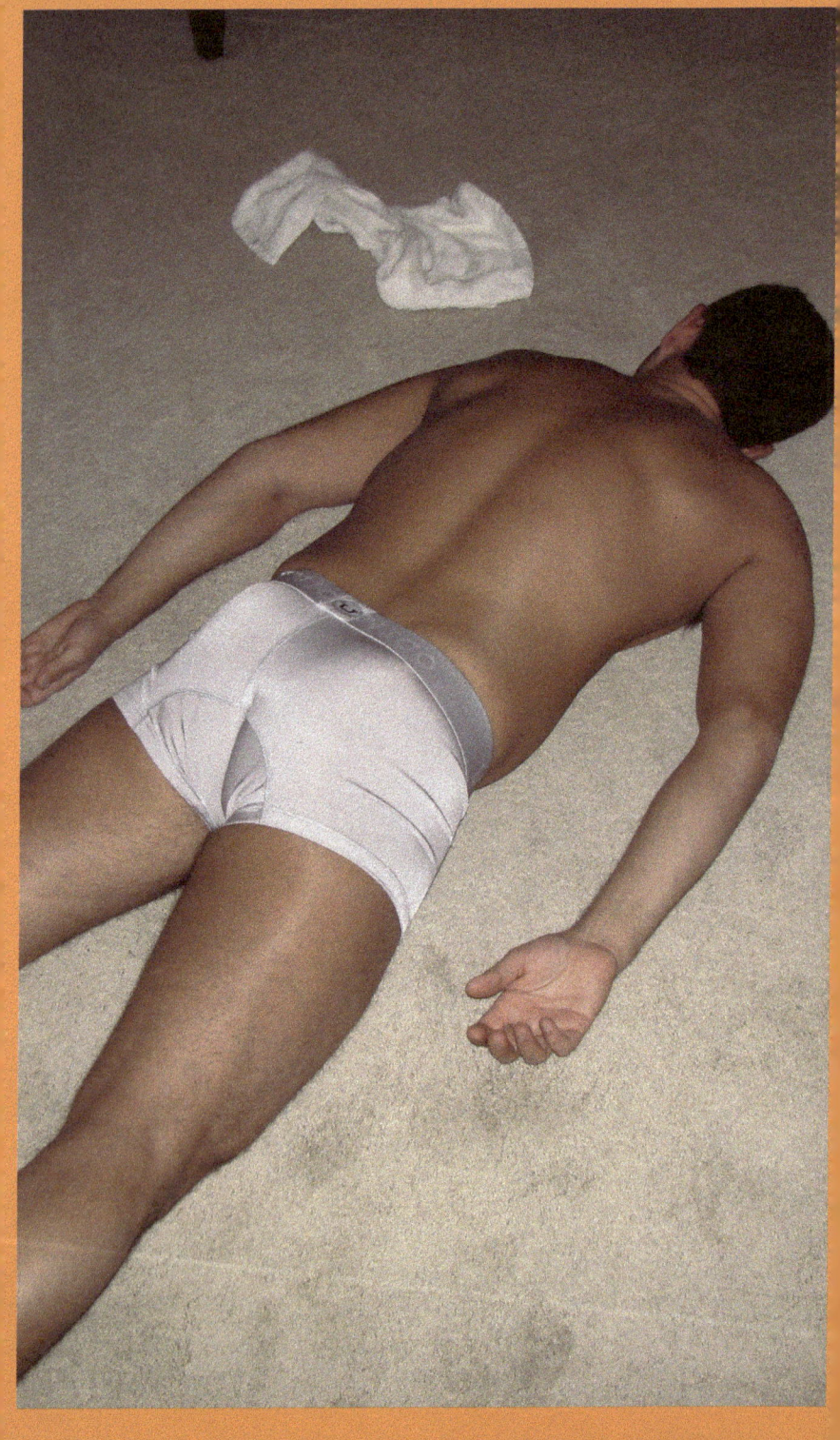

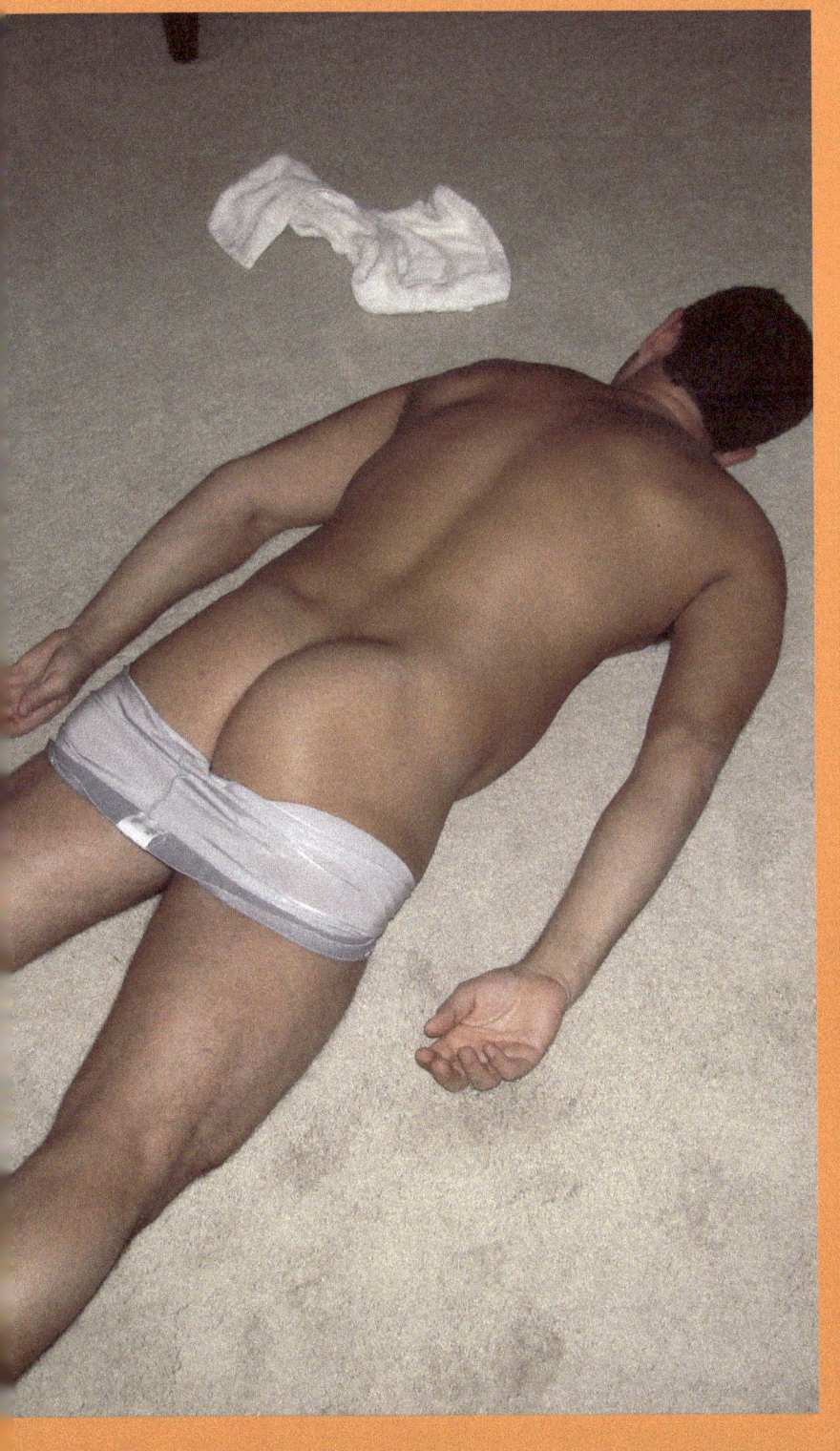

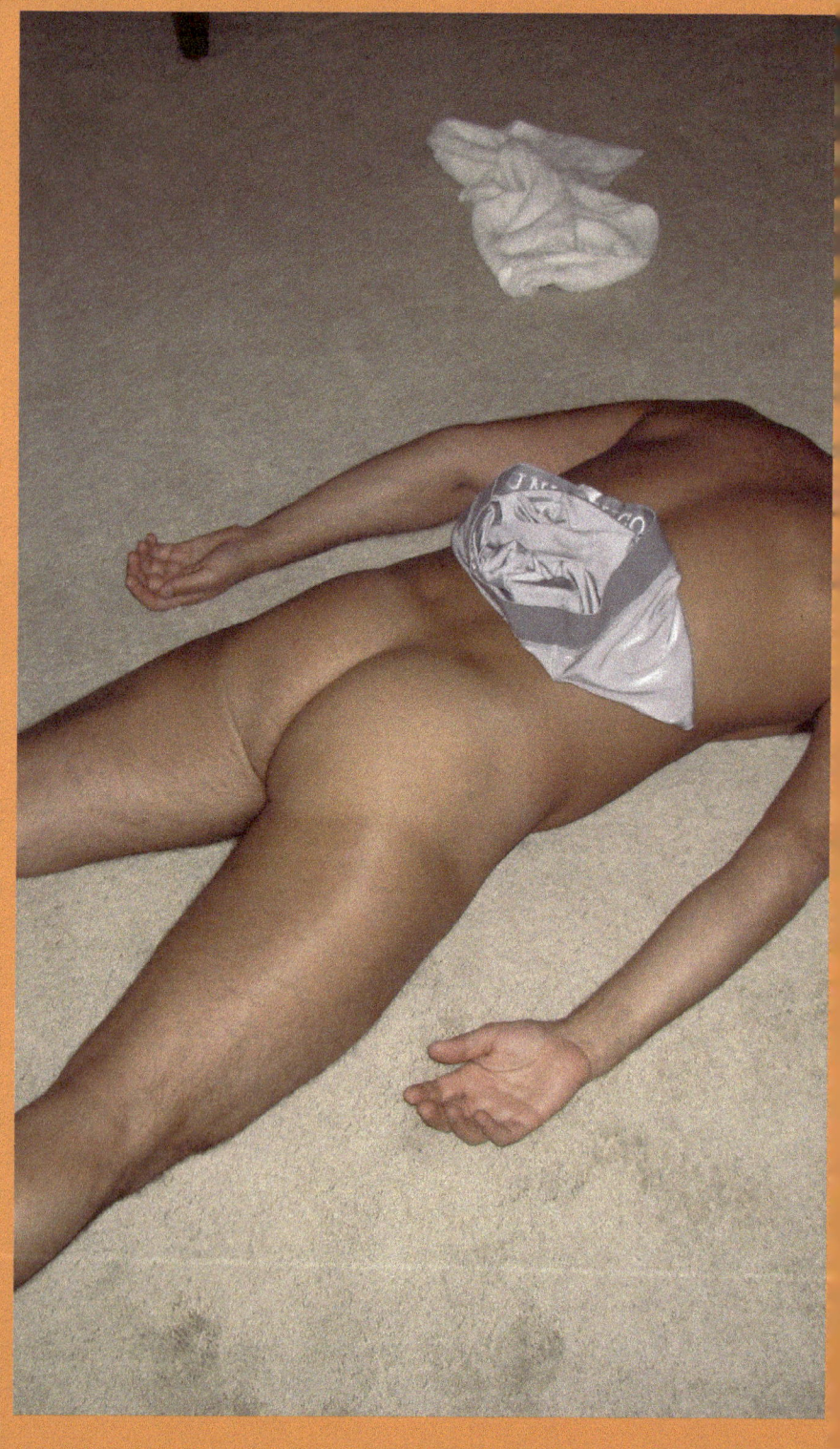

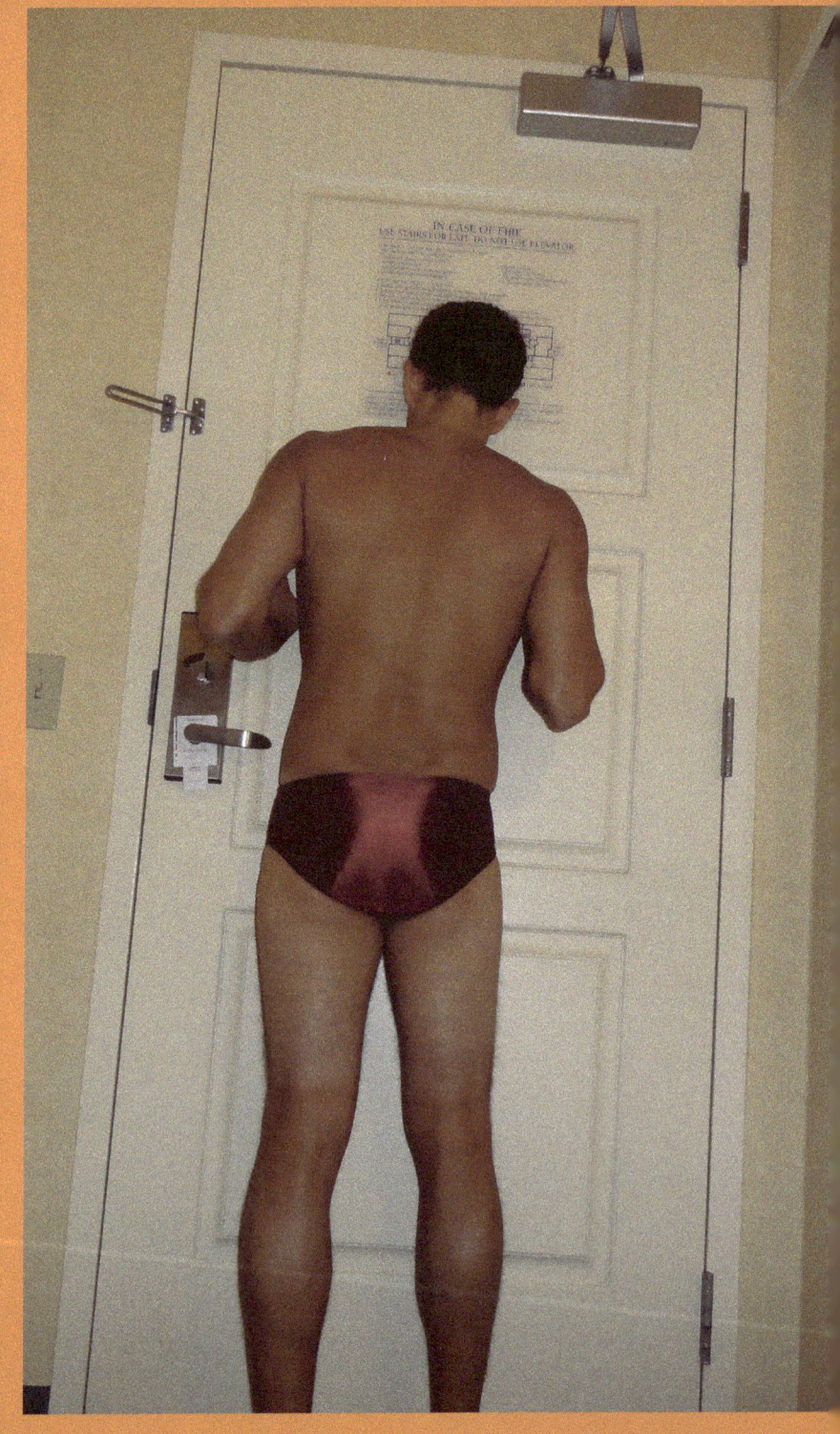

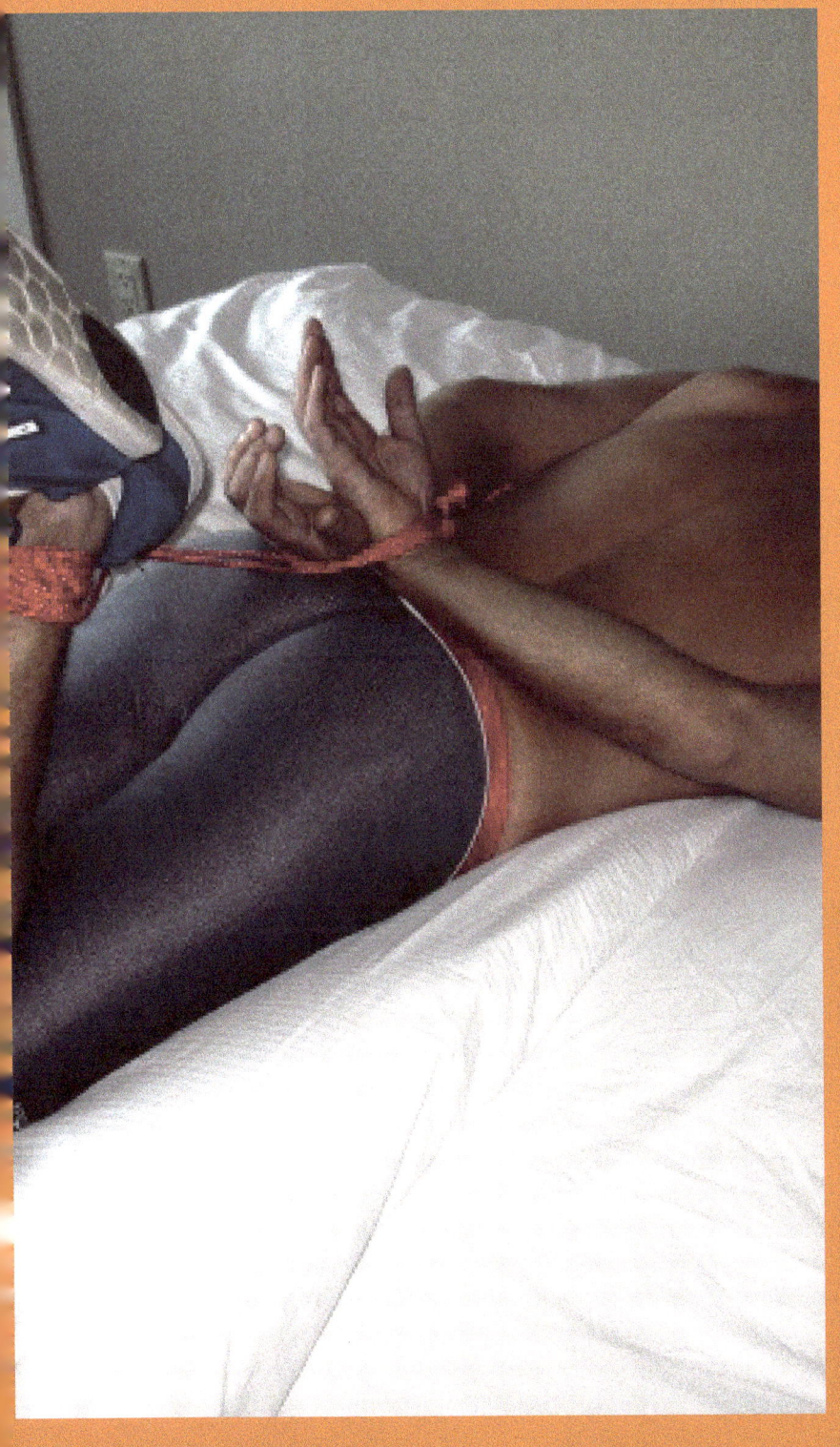

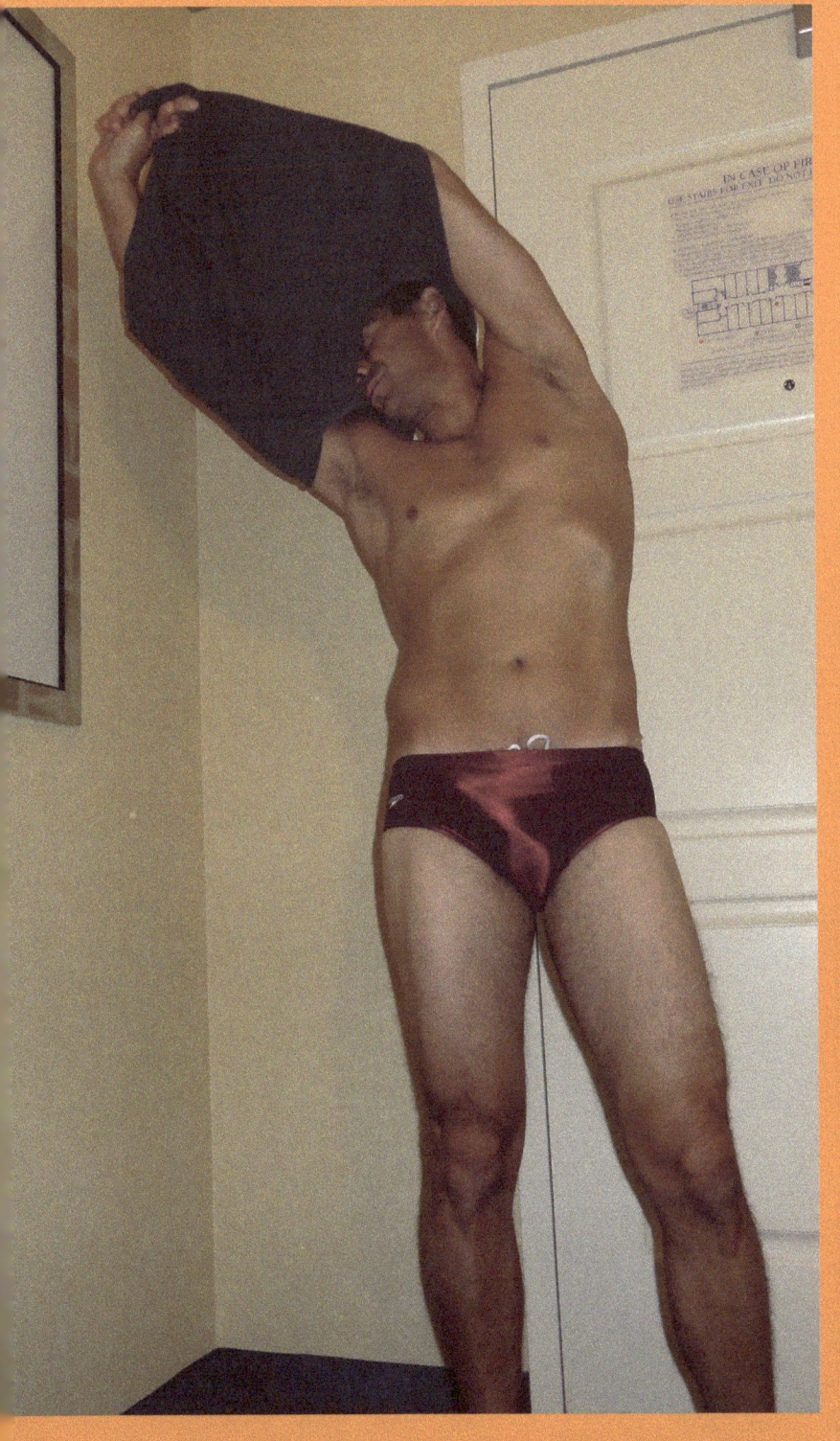

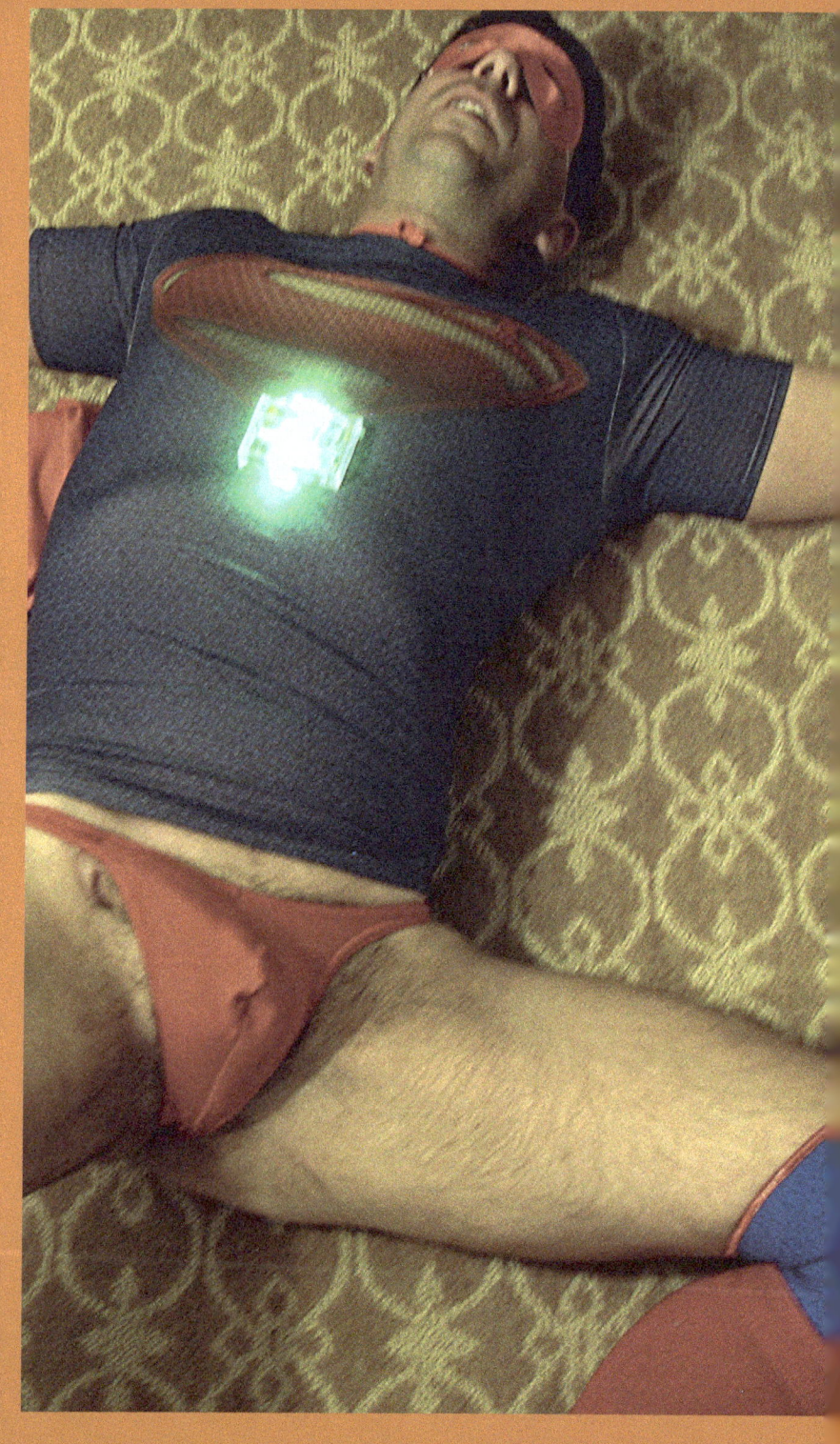

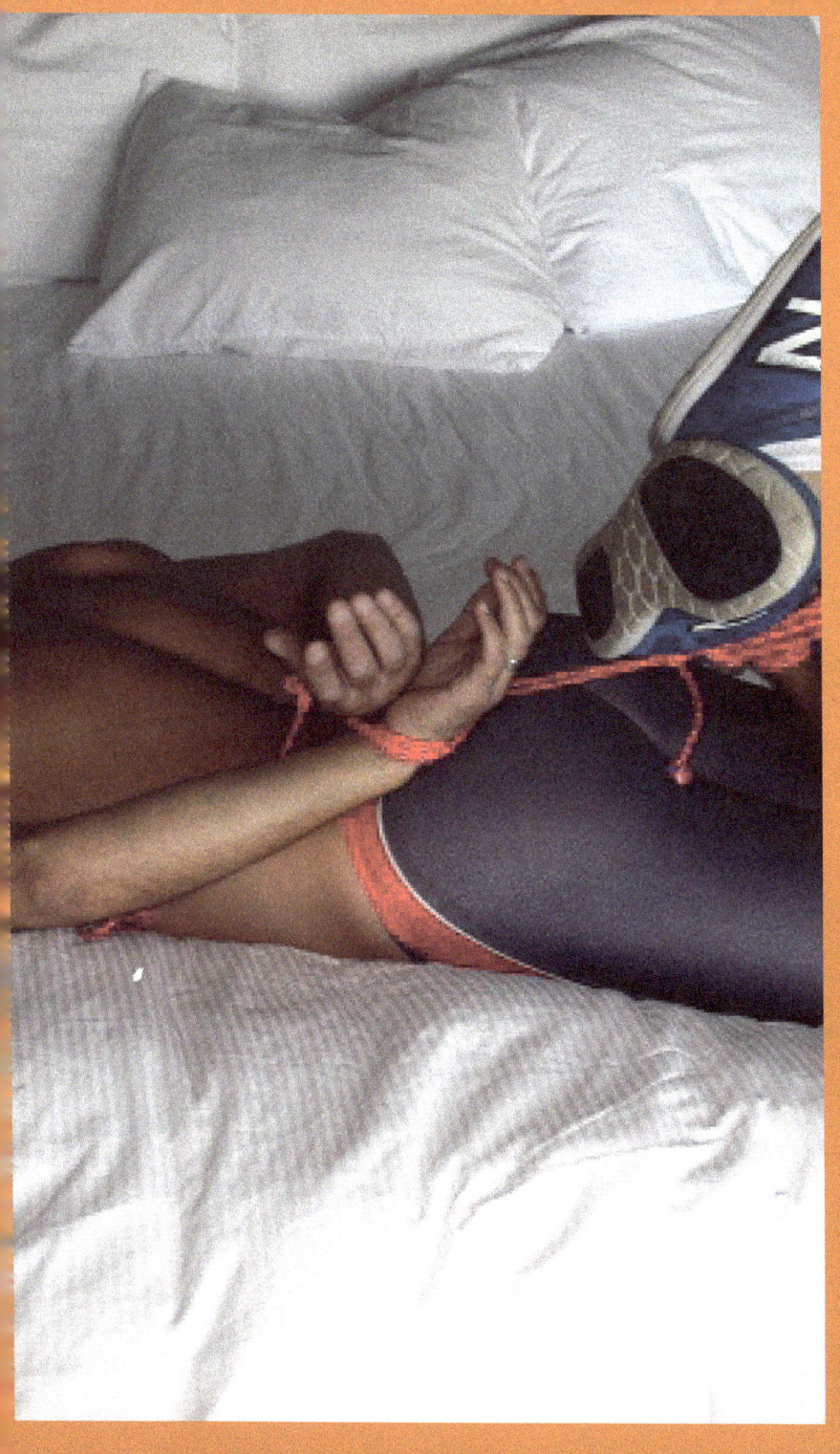

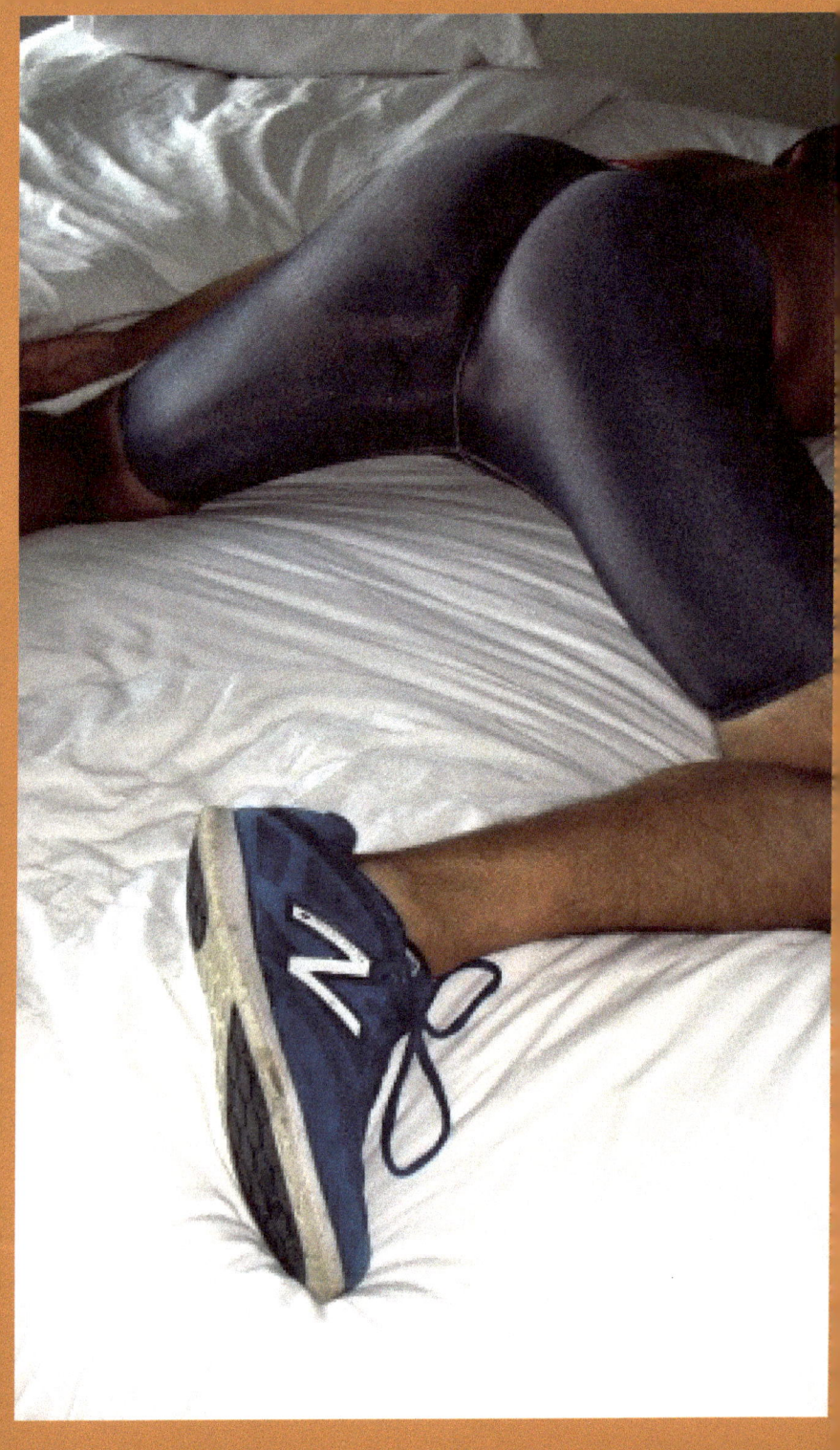

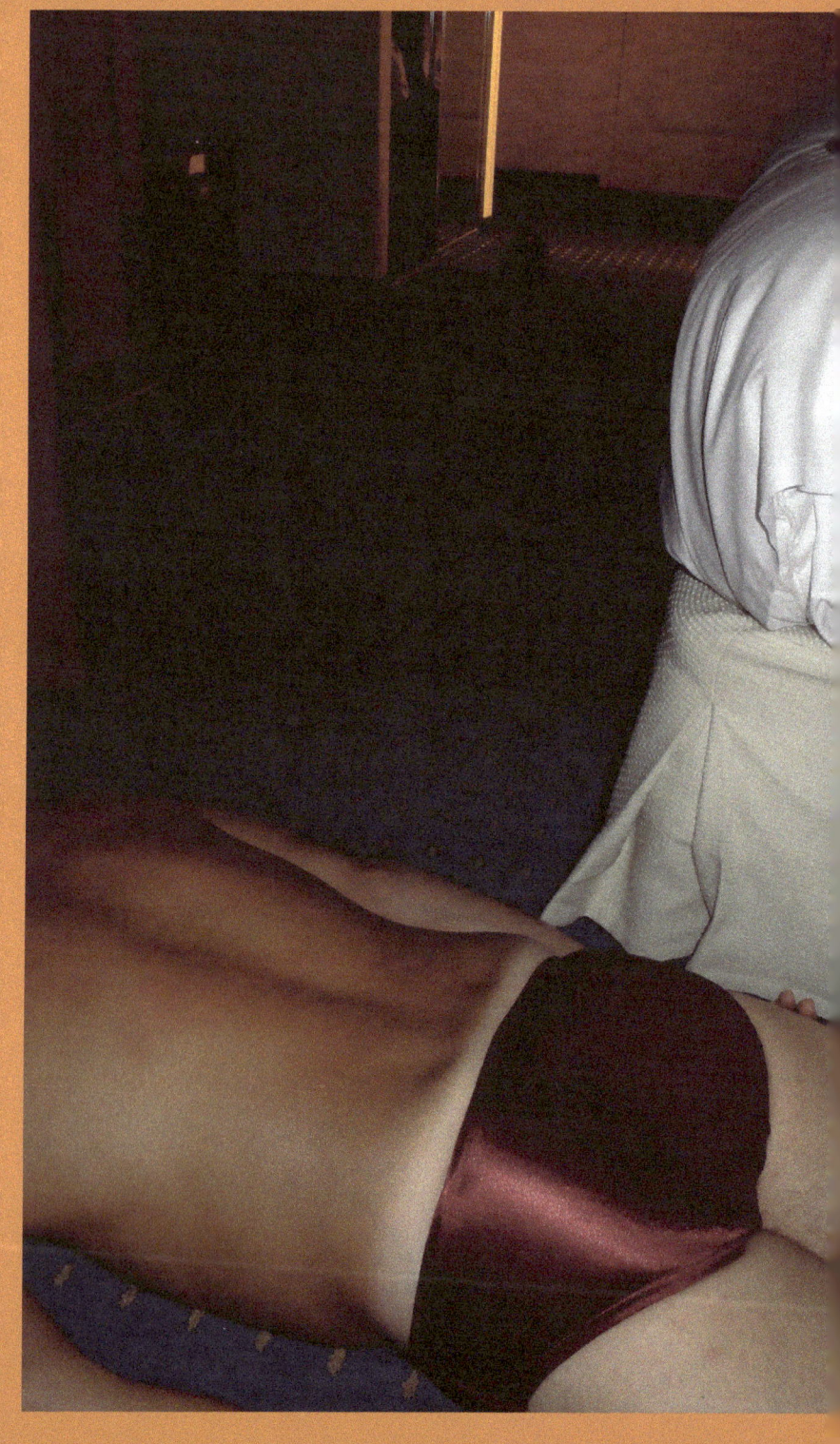

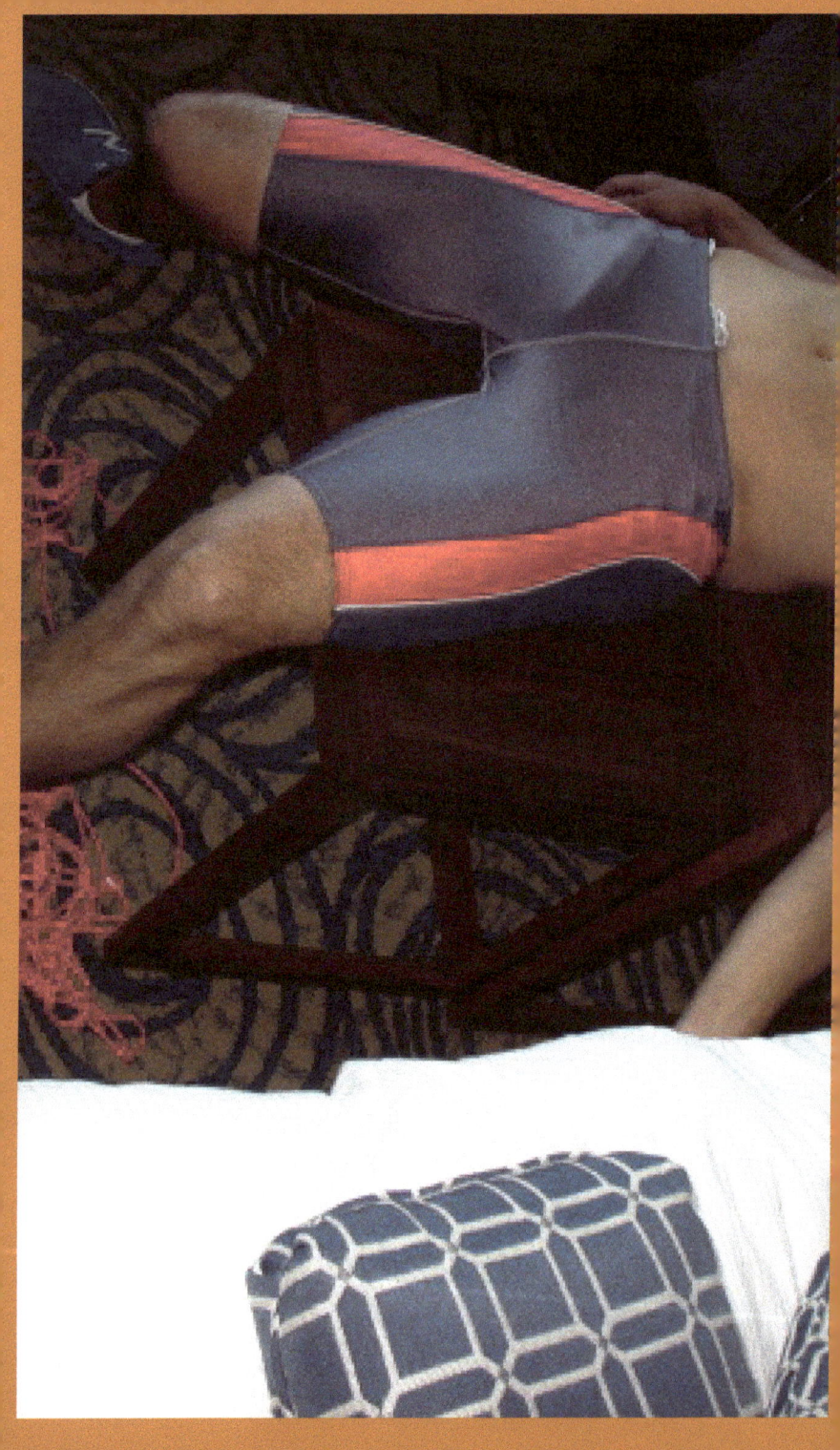

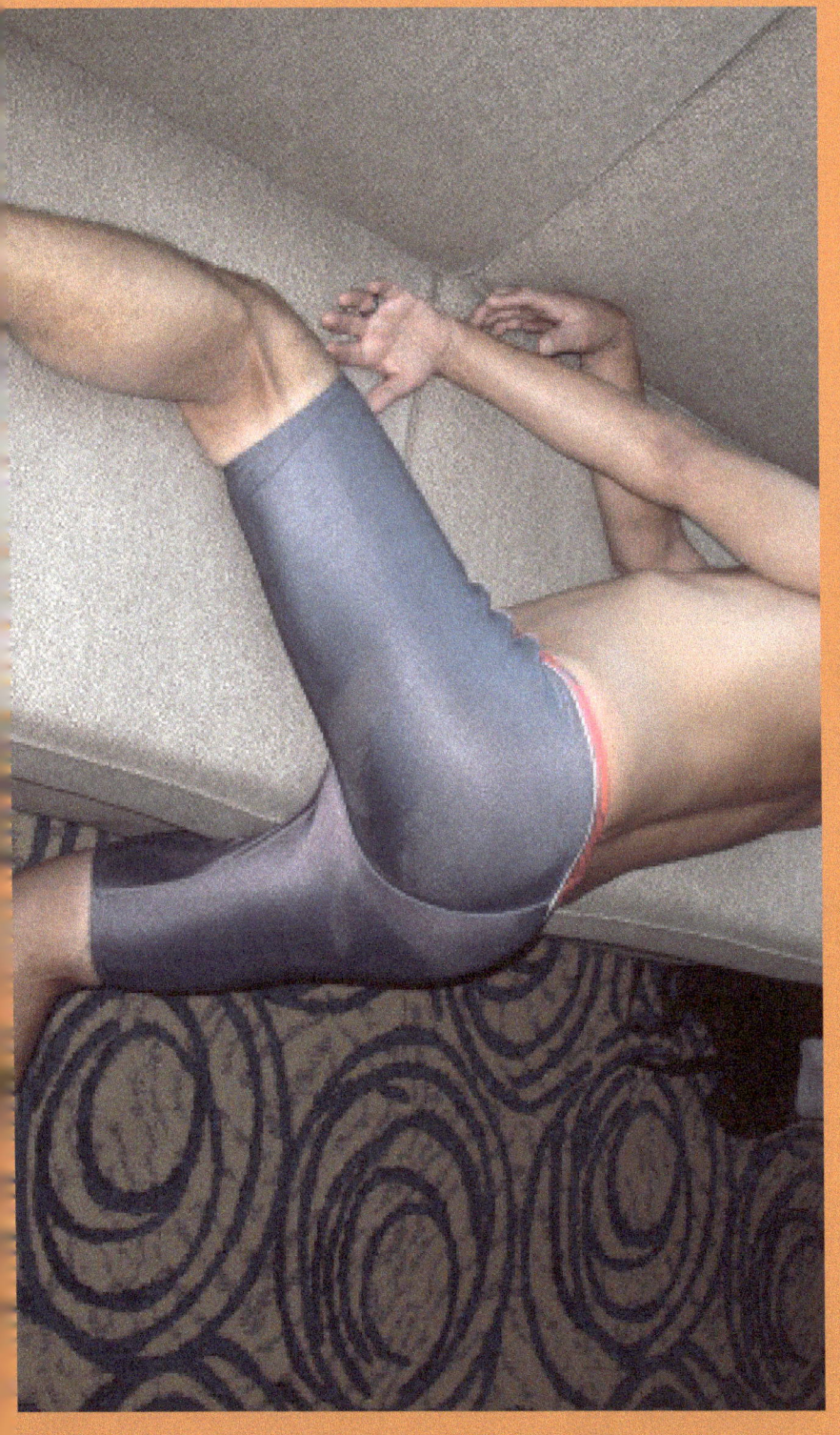

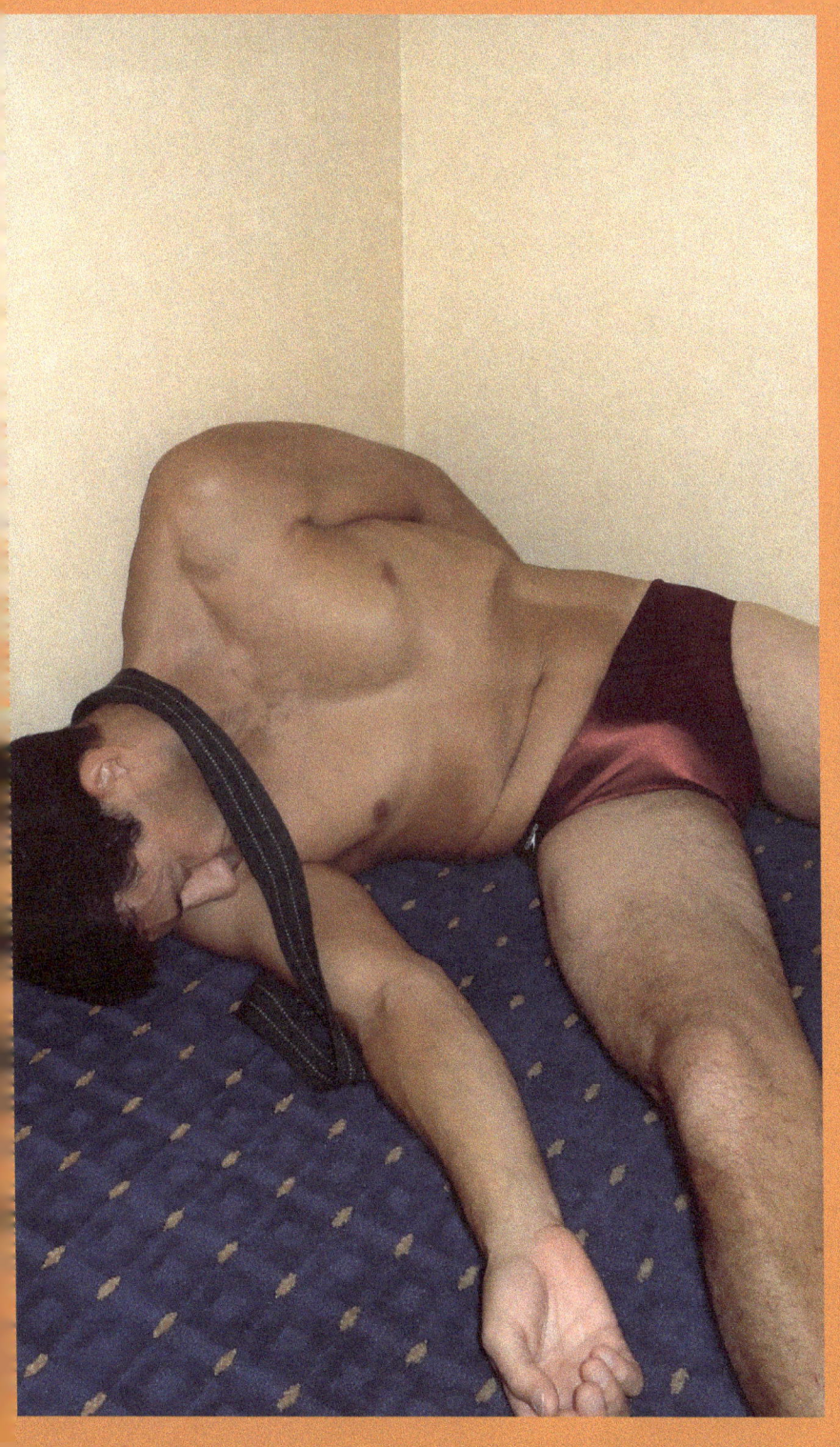

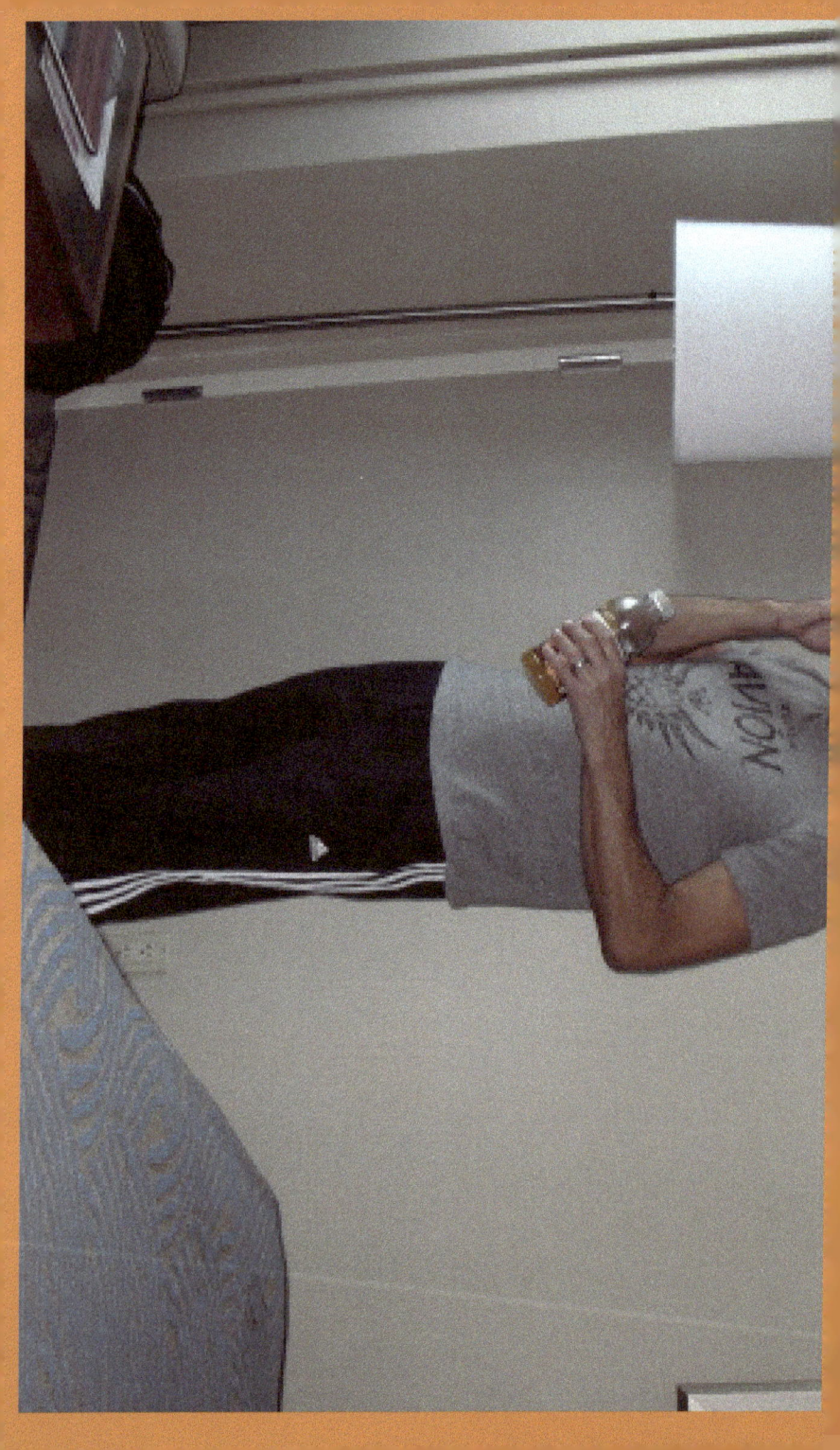

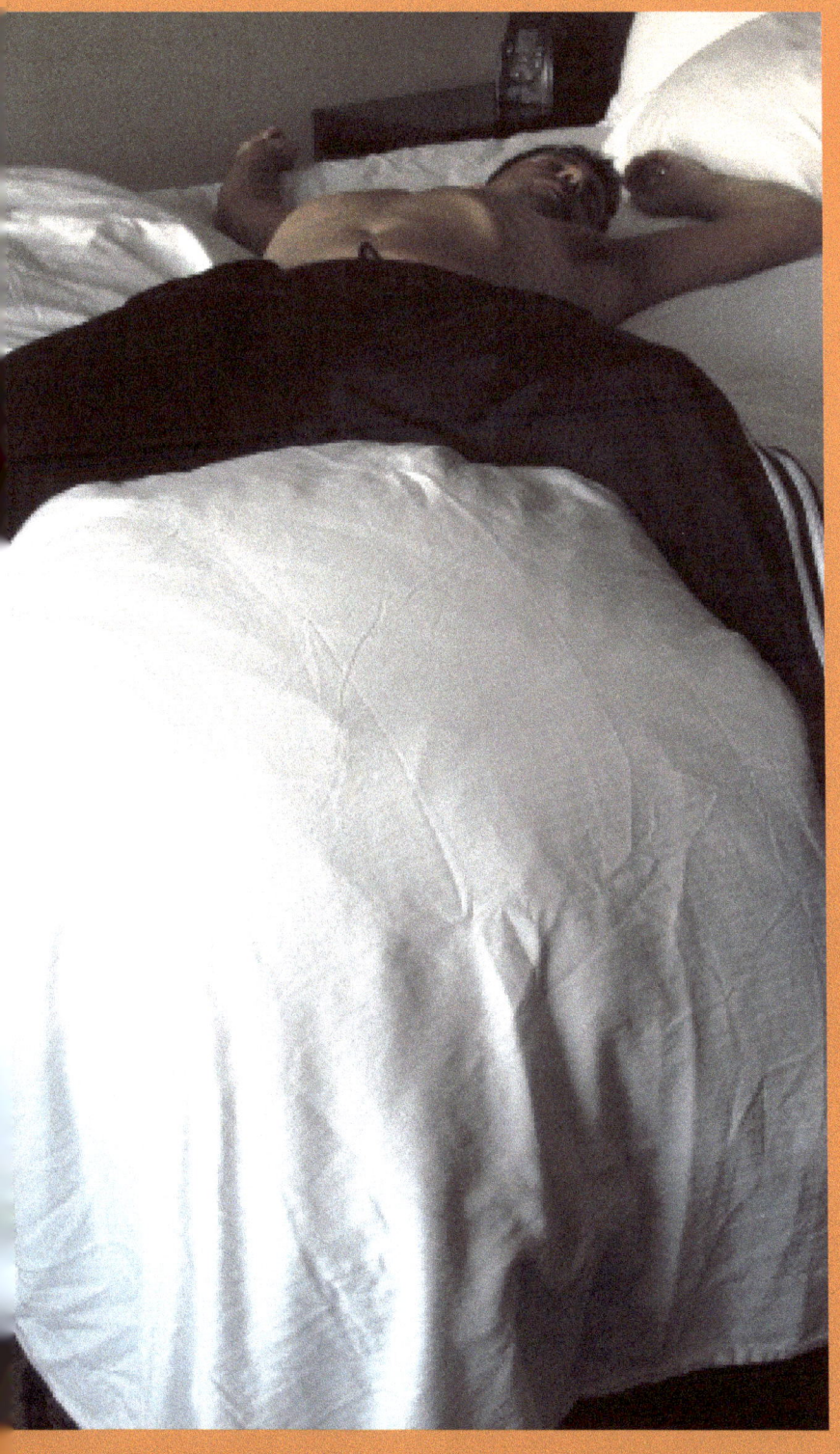

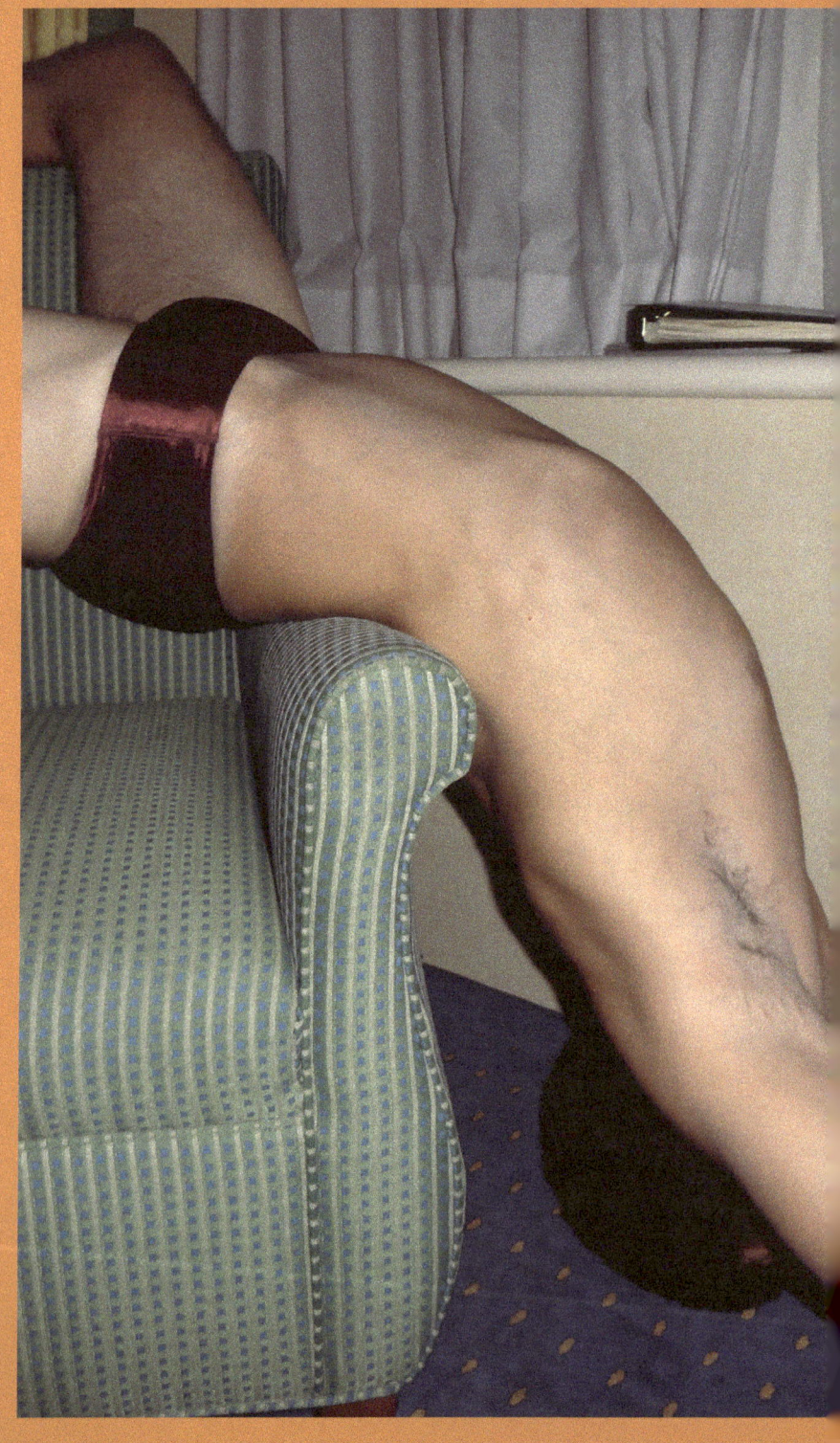